ALEKSANDR A. VOLKOV

EVICTION NOTICE
IN SAN FRANCISCO

Commentaries on elements
necessary to consider
in issuing an eviction notice
in San Francisco

with copious notes and citations

Part I: general elements & for-fault evictions

Part II: general elements of non-fault evictions
and elements of notices for OMI/RMI, sale
after a condo-conversion, demolition and conversion

Second Edition
Version 2.9

VOLF®

2019

CONTINUANCE IN USE. This book is maintained as a private publication of the Volkov Law Office and Aleksandr A. Volkov. No guarantee is given that these materials, either in whole or in any part, will remain available for any particular length of time or will be updated either periodically or ever again. Authors of the materials reserve their rights to disconnect support of this publication at any given moment, without notice.

YOUR FEEDBACK IS REQUESTED. This book is nothing more but an attempt to observe and systematize various rules applicable to making correct and effective eviction notices in San Francisco. The work is far from being complete, it is more at that beginning of its journey, rather than then crossing a finish line. If you have any suggestion on what to add, change, or subtract, please let me know, I will greatly appreciate your feedback. Please send your comments to my email at *alex@volf.com* and put the word "book" in the subject line. Thank you, and I hope you enjoyed reading the book as much as I enjoyed the writing.

DISCLAIMER

A. Volkov. Eviction Notice In San Francisco.

Abbreviations and Terms used in this book:

CFR – U.S. Code of Federal Regulations;

USC – United States Code

HUD – U.S. Department of Housing and Urban Development

SFHA – San Francisco Housing Authority

SFRO – San Francisco Rent Ordinance

CC – California Civil Code

CCP – California Code of Civil Procedure

Cal. Evid. Code – California Evidence Code

Cal. Gov. Code – California Government Code

S.F. Admin. Code – San Francisco Administrative Code

Rent Board – San Francisco Rent Stabilization and Arbitration Board

Rent Ordinance – San Francisco Administrative Code, Chapter 37, also known as the Residential Rent Stabilization and Arbitration Ordinance

Section – Section 37.X of the S.F. Admin. Code, Chapter 37

CONTENTS:

A. Volkov. Eviction Notice In San Francisco.

Table of Contents

INTRODUCTION

Torrance The Tenant stopped paying his rent. Laurence, his landlord, issued a 3-Day Notice to Pay or Quit. Torrance ran to the S.O.S. ("Season Of Sharing[1]") program and the S.O.S. agreed to make a payment on his behalf. Laurence discarded S.O.S. offer as ridiculous and proceeded evicting Torrance in court. Court found for Torrance and further found that Laurence violated the San Francisco Police Code. Eviction failed.

Trevor was causing all kind of nuisance in the house, terrorizing neighbors and causing regular police visits at night. Laurence issued a Notice to Cure or Quit, but did not provide enough specificity for the instances of nuisance. Court found for Trevor and eviction failed.

In the same scenario, after first giving opportunities to cure violations, Laurence issued a Notice to Quit, containing all necessary specifics of the alleged nuisance. Trevor thought he would win since the notice contained no opportunity to cure. Trevor learned in court that not every notice has to have one. Court found for Laurence and Trevor reluctantly vacated.

In almost every eviction, success of the case hangs on the quality of the eviction notice. This book offers a collection of commentaries of what should, or should not, be in that notice so that you won't find yourself on the losing side in your eviction story.

WHAT THIS BOOK IS ABOUT, AN EVICTION NOTICE IN SAN FRANCISCO

An eviction lawsuit (the "unlawful detainer") is administered in a similar way in every county in the state of California. Whether or not the parties are in a municipality where eviction control is enforced, the structure and procedure of the eviction are the same. The difference is in the step before the lawsuit, and that is the step concerned with the eviction notice, a written document served on tenants, informing them that possession of their occupied property is sought for some particular reason, and that an eviction lawsuit may follow if they don't vacate voluntarily within the prescribed time.

This book is about that step, the eviction notice. It is about what should be in it and what should be kept aside, depending on the type of the eviction and laws covering it. Although the particular requirements for an eviction notice come from modern often-changing laws, the basic concept and importance of this step in the eviction process developed over several hundred years.

The procedure of unlawful detainer is a statutory invention, not existed in common law,[2] and it demands strict compliance with the statute. One "who desires to avail himself of the summary remedy provided by this act, must bring himself clearly within its provisions.[2]" The eviction laws of this state are only developing for 150 years, yet most of its legal concepts, including the one concerning an eviction notice, were developed much earlier.

The trespass and breaking into someone's property were recognized as punishable conduct in England as early as in 7th century, according to the "Laws of Æthelberht.[3]" Requirements for notice and for providing an opportunity to cure a "feud," were already present in the 9th century judgments (or "dooms") of Alfred The Great: "we also command: that the man who knows his foe be homesitting fight not before he demand justice of him.[4]"

From Bracton we know that eviction laws and procedures, such as an ejectment and "disseysine," were known in some form in English law since at least the 13th century. A right to recover possession through a "writ of entry," or a lawsuit in an "assise," was executed in many ways similar to the current procedure, including such features as a 5-day period, a delay in eviction afforded to one in a military service, an eviction by writ after judgment, etc.[5] Interestingly, a pre-litigation eviction notice was already required 800 years ago. As early as at the time of Bracton treatise, a predecessor of the modern eviction notice was already in use, then called a "request," required to be made and served before commencement of an eviction lawsuit.[6] It is the service of that request, informing the possessor that "the plaintiff is setting out on his way to sue out a writ against a disseysor," was opening a door to filing a complaint, or, as Bracton puts it, tendering the tenement litigious.[7]

During Bracton times, and most likely for a few centuries before, a peaceful eviction lawsuit was only an alternative, equally available with a co-existing practice of recovering the land by force, then a preferable course of action when the wrongful possession was itself obtained by force. The practice of using force was later outlawed, starting the development of English statutes of forcible entry and unlawful detainer since 1328.[8]

A. Volkov. Eviction Notice In San Francisco.

California had adopted its own "Forcible Entry and Detainer Act" soon after the state's formation. The original act did not require the notice, and was not instructing as to its length, yet its necessity was adopted from the case law.[9] The Act, as amended by the third section of the Act of 1862, enforced the requirement to substitute formal entry with a written demand.[10]

At the time of those legislature innovations, the City and County of San Francisco was already experiencing fast growth and its residents fought in court for the land rights. On September 21, 1849, William Taylor arrived to San Francisco and observed the following:

> "[W]e stopped and took a view of the city of tents. Not a brick house in the place, and but few wooden ones, and not a wharf or pier in the harbor. But for a few old adobe houses, it would have been easy to imagine that the whole city was pitched the evening before … and I felt oppressed with the fear that … those tents might all be struck some morning, and the city suddenly leave its moorings for parts unknown.[11]"

Already during the next year, dozens of eviction cases reached appellate level.[12] The second-ever recorded San Francisco case was about a tenant successfully challenging an eviction, including on the grounds of lack of notice.[13] It was decided in March of 1850.

Fast forward to our times, land and housing in San Francisco are still hot topics, if not the hottest. It seems today that every political, economical, or social issue in this town is explained through the prism of battling interests of landlords and tenants. Each team has its champions, support groups, advocates, and a safety net of sources offered to help. The main battlefield where landlords and tenants are bound to disagree is, of course, the eviction process. And that's the process, where no amount of help is enough.

Whenever the parties, landlord or tenant, will attempt to educate themselves on the legal requirements and steps of a particular eviction, they will soon face two considerable bumps on their learning path: the fact that there are several routs through which the applicable law is developed, and that there is no one single organization informing the public on all the requirements.

There are several routs, because, while evictions in the County of San Francisco are covered by the applicable state and Federal laws, there is also a body of city-specific municipal law, applicable to almost every housing situation happening here and different in one way or another from the state of Federal rules. And there is no one single organization to help public with all the relevant rules and issues. There is the "Rent Board,[14]" which manages most of the relevant portions of the municipal code related to evictions, such as the San Francisco Rent Ordinance,[15] but that is not all-inclusive: other portions of the San Francisco municipal codes (Health Code, Planning Code, Police Code, Codes of the San Francisco Building Inspection Commission) and their corresponding regulatory departments may apply. San Francisco residential rent laws and regulations are multilayered and therefore complicated, sometimes to a confusing degree.

While the Rent Board is a valuable tool for both tenants and landlords, it does not cover every angle of the process, nor may it provide a legal advice. This is why it will be beneficial for landlords and tenants to obtain legal representation and rely on a recommendation of their counsel. Yet the first step in any eviction, the issuance of an eviction notice, is often done by the property owners or managers before an attorney gets involved. The requirements are complex, and the notices issued without professional oversight are often prone for an attack for non-compliance. As a result, too many a case are built on a weak foundation, with defects revealed when it is late, or even too late, to fix. This book aims to arm its readers with enough guidance to recognize notice compliance issues early and more fully.

There is another reason why this book focuses on eviction notices rather than evictions as a whole—it is the intricacy of laws and regulations, many specific only to the city and county of San Francisco. The landlord is required to abide strictly with all applicable rules or will risk not only the loss of the case and failure to recover the property, but also to incur potential penalties or even a counter action for wrongful eviction. This web of interrelated regulations plays a main role at the notice level and the notice has to be perfected *before* the eviction lawsuit filed with the court. Once the lawsuit is filed, it is (i) administered primarily by state-wide laws, (ii) landlords are more commonly assisted in that process by an attorney, (iii) the jurisdiction of the municipal administrative bodies, such as the Rent Board, ceases, and (iv) ... it is too late to fix either the notice or the service of it.

The eviction notice is the Rosetta stone of almost every eviction, particularly so in San Francisco.[16] Without a proper notice, an eviction where notice is required has a high chance to fail. I hope the information gathered here will prove itself helpful for the landlords to make their notices right from the first time, and for the tenants to educate themselves on how to successfully defend against noncompliant evictions.

In our journey through the potential eviction scenarios, we'll take a ground-up approach, looking at the problem from the perspective of that apartment or a house, rather than from the state legislature chambers or a Congress standpoint. Since what's closer to home affects the process more, this approach seems deserving most of the attention.

This book is primarily structured by the enumerated types of eviction acknowledged in the Rent Ordinance, because this way covers almost all evictions possible in San Francisco. The book starts with explaining some general steps and observations, as well as evictions not covered by the Rent Ordinance. The second and third sections address particulars for the notices issued for each of the evictions allowed under the Rent Ordinance, organized here in the same order as they are addressed in the Ordinance. This publication covers all for-fault grounds and the first four non-fault grounds (OMI, RMI, due to the sale after a condo-conversion, and for demolition or removal from housing use), with intent to update and complete it with remaining non-fault grounds in later additions.

A reader facing a particular type of eviction will be able to proceed directly to the applicable chapter, while keeping a finger on the chapters covering general observations, and get the coverage of that eviction type without reading the entire book. I aimed at making it more of a reference list than a cohesive reading, and I feel the goal would be achieved if my book finds its place on readers' desks more often than on shelves.

WHAT THIS BOOK IS NOT ABOUT

Each real property is unique.[17] And so are unique each eviction's particular facts. It follows that the eviction notice ought to be unique as well. Nothing can substitute an informed professional advice, based on particular circumstances of the case. This is why the purpose of this book is not to replace an attorney, or even to cover the entire scope of the eviction laws, but to assist a reader in research on a particular type of a residential eviction taken place in San Francisco.

The goal of the book is to cover eviction notices issued for each of the just causes listed in the Rent Ordinance. Since the Rent Ordinance only covers residential leases, the material in this book does not cover notices for terminating commercial tenancies, as well as for terminating those residential tenancies, which might be exempt from the Rent Ordinance coverage. Those exemptions are listed in more detail in the next chapter.

This book also does not cover what particular facts give grounds to what particular kind of eviction, or any eviction at all. While some seem to be fairly obvious (if the tenant does not pay rent, the notice should be for non-payment of rent), some require detailed analysis before a decision can be made that the grounds for an eviction exist. For instance, it is not that obvious to define what constitutes "nuisance." It requires many more factors to consider when an owner move-in eviction or an Ellis Act eviction is appropriate. Even for a seemingly simple decision in a non-payment of rent case, it is not always straightforward—there are situations when the tenant is justified in paying less or no rent.[18]

PREAMBLE TO SECOND EDITION

While the second part of the book (covering non-fault eviction notices) is being prepared, the first part has been already republished in several versions and editions. The second edition had to come out due to substantial updates of the Rent Ordinance with passing of Ordinance 171-15 in 2015, and then again, updates taken place in 2017, including a major re-write of the owner-move-in regulations effective January 1, 2018. The part about the general elements applicable to all notices and the first four non-fault evictions, being already completed, was also included, starting from version 2.4. Several chapters and applicable rules had to be changed to avoid obsolescence. As Emperor Justinian himself found out 1500 years ago, the shelf life of a law review is short (his Corpus Juris Civil becoming obsolete immediately upon completion).[19] This is still true today, especially when it covers the law of interest and active discussion of as robust a community as San Francisco. The most I can hope for this publication is to remain useful to its readers for at least a year since its release, and with that goal in mind I made thorough updates in almost every chapter.

EXEMPTIONS FROM THE EVICTION CONTROL

In general, the variety of ways to recover real property by means of a lawsuit is quite broad. Not all of those actions require a preceding notice, not every eviction is subject to the eviction control, and even a lesser pool of properties falls within the eviction control under the Rent Ordinance.

Someone unwanted could be on the property for other reasons, for no reason, or under a different kind of agreement than a lease. It could be a trespasser,[20] a licensee,[21] a guest,[22] a co-owner,[23] an adversary possessor,[24] a "tenant at sufferance,[25]" or those who hold the property "[b]y force, or by menaces and threats of violence.[26]" Procedures to remove persons from a property in such situations are available, such as an action in ejectment,[27] injunction,[28] an action for trespass,[29] recovery after abandonment,[30] an action for forcible entry and detainer,[31] an action for quiet title,[32] and alike, but these procedures are not part of this book, for the main reason that above mentioned actions require no notice in compliance with the San Francisco Rent Ordinance.[33] The law covering those procedures is uniform statewide and has no special or different treatment in San Francisco.

Even termination of some San Francisco tenancies is still exempt from the Rent Ordinance. The Rent Ordinance primarily defines exemptions in Sections 37.2, 37.3, and 37.9 of the San Francisco Administrative Code.[34]

Tenancies Fully Exempt

Post-1979 properties and single-family units are *not* unconditionally or fully exempt, read Nos. (6)–(8), (10), (11), (14)–(16) below. There are only three types of tenancies truly exempt:

(1) Non-residential tenancies are generally fully exempt,[35] except when used for residential purposes.[36]

(2) Also exempt are "dwelling units in non-profit cooperatives owned, occupied and controlled by a majority of the residents or dwelling units solely owned by a non-profit public benefit corporation governed by a board of directors the majority of which are residents of the dwelling units and where it is required in the corporate by-laws that rent increases be approved by a majority of the residents." Section 37.2(r)(2).

(3) The same is true to the "housing accommodations in any hospital, convent, monastery, extended care facility, asylum, residential care or adult day health care facility for the elderly which must be operated pursuant to a license issued by the California Department of Social Services, as required by California Health and Safety Chapters 3.2 and 3.3, or in dormitories owned and operated by an institution of higher education, a high school, or an elementary school." Section 37.2(r)(3).

(4) The San Francisco Rent Board's "Fact Sheet 1[37]" lists 11 categories of units fully exempt, although not all of them explained or supported by a cited authority. The list is almost an exact copy of the same categories listed in Rent Board's "Topic No. 017.[38]" I can't agree with the entire scope of 11 exemptions. For instance, it lists units "that have been permanently removed from rental housing use pursuant to the Ellis Act" (*Id.*, ¶8). I think such units still can be re-rented, and, if the new occupant would possess such unit for 32+ days, that unit will again become subject to the Rent Ordinance. Another suspicious category there is under ¶10, "[c]ommercial space where there is incidental and infrequent residential use."

Tenancies Partially Exempt

(5) Tenancies under a contract with a government agency for subsidized housing, such as the SFHA, are partially exempt and still require a notice.[39] Section 37.2(r)(4). Exemptions from this exclusion are listed as sub-sections (A)—(C) of Section 37.2(r)(4), potentially bringing some of those tenancies back under the eviction control. Despite being otherwise excluded, these programs have their own requirements, such as different grounds for termination,[40] different time periods for some kinds of the notices (90-days,[41] twelve and six months[42]), service of copy of the notice on the agency,[43] additional mandatory disclosures to the tenant.[44]

There are different types of the so-called "Section 8" rent subsidy programs: a certificate program and various kinds of voucher programs.[45] "In the certificate program, the rental subsidy is generally based on the actual rent of a unit leased by the assisted family. In the voucher program, the rental subsidy is determined by a formula.[46]" Most voucher programs are either rent-based or income-based.[47] Those vouchers, where the voucher program establishes "the tenant's share of base rent as a fixed percentage of a tenant's income," are exempt.[48] Other vouchers are not exempt (*Id.*) The certificate program is also not exempt.[49] Even the exempt vouchers still put a 5-year cap on the maximum rent to be charged in the future, after a landlord terminates the subsidy contract.[50]

(6) Tenancies in the newer buildings, ones "for which a certificate of occupancy was first issued after the effective date of this ordinance." Section 37.2(r)(5). "[T]he effective date of this ordinance" is generally understood as referring to the date of June 13, 1979.[51] However, the effective date of applying the exemptions of 37.2 is August 24, 1980,[52] which would only be material for the leases commenced before that date.

Three types of rental units are *not* included in the exemption under Section 37.2(r)(5): properties developed pursuant to a development agreement with the city under the S.F. Admin Code, Section 56, even though these are rental units built later than the effective date of the Ordinance[53]; properties, to which the title had passed by means of foreclosure or a sale under the defaulted deed of trust[54]; and properties defined under Section 37.3(d) as "Separately Alienable Parcels."

(7) This last category under Sec. 37.3(d), "Separately Alienable Parcels," is itself an exception, covered in sub-section Sec. 37.2(r)(7) (dedicated for the "Costa-Hawkins Act"). Although its title implies to deal with separate parcels, the definition of the exemption covers "a dwelling or a unit which is alienable separate from the title to any other dwelling unit.[55]" In other words, a subject dwelling or a rental unit has to be on a separate parcel from another dwelling or rental unit to be exempt. Therefore, a mix-use property, where is only one residential unit (or only one commercial unit used for residential purposes), and the rest of the property is not residential, will be exempt under 37.3(d)(1)(A) from the rent control.

Exemption provided under Sec. 37.3(d) is not without limitations. It excludes from the scope of the exemption units where exists "serious health, safety, fire, or building code violations,[56]" or where a previous tenancy was terminated under CC §§ 827, 1946, or 1946.1.[57] Thus, properties otherwise exempt under the definition of Section 37.3(d)(1)(A) may still remain not exempt, due to the units' condition. 37.3(d)(1)(C).[58]

The San Francisco Rent Board provides more insight on partial exemptions for the Costa-Hawkins and Government-Subsidized properties in Fact Sheet 1,[37] and Topics Nos. 018 and 019.[59]

(8) Tenancies in a building "which has undergone substantial rehabilitation after the effective date of this ordinance." Section 37.2(r)(6). This sub-section has its own exceptions: "RAP" units,[60] and pre-foreclosure tenancies.[61] At the same time, it does not mention limitations imposed on the new buildings, specified under the 37.2(r)(5) immediately above. This leads to an unexpected conclusion that older buildings substantially renovated after June 13, 1979, enjoy more freedom from eviction control than the buildings built entirely anew after the same date.

(9) Tenancies created under the Good Samaritan exclusion, Section 37.2(a)(1)(D), are exempt under the rules stated in the section.

(10) "An owner who resides in the same rental unit with his or her tenant.[62]" This exemption appears to apply only when there is just one tenant: "[i]f the owner rents to more than one roommate, the court may find that each room in the unit constitutes a separate rental unit; in such cases, the owner will need a just cause reason under the Ordinance to evict each of the roommates."
(Topic No. 210,[62] *supra*.) An owner does not have to inform the tenant about this exception prior to tenant's move-in. As confirmed in 2019 *Chun v. Del Cid* decision decided based on LA ordinance, the court indeed may find that leasing by rooms may make a single-family residence subject to the rent control regulations as a multi-unit arrangement; property's original design does not control the exception.[63]

(11) A roommate tenancy commenced on or after May 25, 1998, where a master tenant (who is not an owner of record of the subject property) informed the tenant in writing, before tenant's moving-in, "that the tenancy is not subject to the just cause provisions of Section 37.9.[64]" This exemption also appears to apply only when there is just one roommate.[62] Unlike the similar owner's exception above, a master tenant does have to inform the roommate about this exception prior to roommate's move-in.

(12) Hotels and short-term "accommodations," for less than 32 continuous days *appear* to be exempt under Section 37.2(r)(1), but often these tenancies are not exempt, such as when a tenant is moved from one unit to another by same landlord in periods shorter than 32 days. Evictions from these units are allowed only for the Rent Ordinance's just causes, or the landlord will have to overcome a presumption of playing "musical chairs." "An eviction for a purpose not permitted under Sec. 37.9(a) shall be deemed to be an action to recover possession in order to avoid having a unit come within the provisions of this Chapter." Section 37.2(r)(1).

(13) Depending on the circumstances, housing provided as part of wage compensation may be exempt from the Rent Ordinance.[65]

Tenancies Not Exempt

(14) "In law" units are generally *not* exempt.[66] See also, relevant analysis of the original design of the property not controlling, under exception No. 10, above, and the *Chun v. Del Cid* decision.

(15) Newly added units under the "Addition of Dwelling Units" or ADU program, initiated in March 2015 Ordinance 30-15 (Sup. Wiener) and then amended by Ordinances Nos. 162-16, 95-17, 162-17, are generally not exempt and subject to rent control, per specific contract between the property owner and the City, waiving otherwise applicable Costa-Hawkins exemption.[67]

(16) Foreclosed units are not exempt; property ownership transfer through foreclosure provides additional protection, event to some tenancies previously and otherwise exempt (tenancies discussed above, under partially exempt scenarios Nos. 6, 7, and 8).

Under the common law, the grantor (an original landlord) could grant realty rights, including leasehold, only from the "bundle of rights" she had in that property. Thus, if a landlord had the property secured by a deed of trust or mortgage, and such security had priority over the lease, foreclosing on that security would terminate landlord's rights in the property and, consequently, the rights of anyone who claimed the property through or under that landlord, such as her tenants.

The "Protecting Tenants Against Foreclosure Act of 2009[68]" changed this rule and "causes a bona fide lease for a term to survive foreclosure through the end of the lease.[69]" In San Francisco, a special chapter was added to the Rent Ordinance, addressing foreclosure evictions, Section 37.9D. This chapter adds protections, event to the tenancies previously exempt:

  - tenancies otherwise exempt from the eviction control coverage (Sec. 37.2(r)(5), (6), or (7)), may not be terminated post-foreclosure except for the just causes for eviction specified in the Ordinance.[70]

- if the new landlord fails to deliver two proscribed notices[71] to the tenants in the foreclosed property, this failure becomes a defense against an eviction.[72]

GENERAL PREREQUISITE: LANDLORD-TENANT RELATIONSHIP

"The ordinance does not require that the landlord-tenant relationship be initiated by the parties for such a relationship to exist,[73]" but an existing landlord-tenant relationship is a prerequisite for issuing most of the notices covered in this book. Aside from one cause for eviction, Sec. 37.9(a)(7),[74] materials here are only useful if that relationship is present, and thus terminable by the eviction notice. The relationship is most often manifested in a lease agreement, in one form or another.

So, step one is to determine if the lease agreement exists. As it is with a general contract, the lease contract can be expressed or implied, oral or written,[75] and it has to reflect "that the parties intend to create a landlord-tenant relationship and must contain the following: a designation of the parties, a description of the premises, the rent to be paid, the time and manner of payment, and the term for which the tenant will rent the property... Provisions for the payment of rent and a transfer of use and possession of property are essential elements of a lease.[76]"

If there is no written lease, or the lease document lacks any of the elements stated above, consider if other writings can help with establishing necessary facts. Several written documents can be construed together as a contract,[77] such as the tenant's estoppel certificate.[78]

For instance, rent payment checks can supplement many of the facts: they usually contain both parties' signatures, they have the amount, they may have useful references made in the "Memo" field, they have the dates of payment (and a series of checks may show parties' customary conduct in handling payments over a period of time). It may even have a property description, as an address printed under the payor's name. Courts had found a written and signed check as a sufficient acceptance of the terms of the contract.[79]

A lease might be oral, but the eviction notice must be made in writing.[80]

Defining the lease terms is a necessary prerequisite. You need to know the terms to see if any of them were violated. You also need to know the terms for creating any of the eviction notices, and to see if the eviction is warranted at all, if it fits any of the allowed just causes under the Rent Ordinance,[81] or exempt from its provisions.[82] For both sides of the relationship, the better the terms are defined, the easier it is to follow them or to determine if any of the terms were breached. "[f]or certaintie is the mother of quietnesse and repose, and incertaintie the cause of variance and contentions," says Sir Edward Coke.[83]

Don't treat this chapter as covering *all* necessary or recommended terms for a lease agreement. Many more shall or should be included in the San Francisco lease agreement, *e.g.*, a clause regarding subletting,[84] or the recently enacted smoking policy disclosure.[85]

If you are creating a new tenancy, consider that, in an unfortunate but possible event of an eviction in the future, the written lease agreement will be most likely the "Exhibit 1" of a verified complaint.[86] Anything said or omitted in the lease may be later used against you.

Regardless of the grounds, if the tenant is entitled to a pre-litigation eviction notice (cases not requiring a notice are mentioned above and are not subject of this book), such notice has to have several elements present on its face to be valid.

Consider also that, in the following eviction action, the notice and its service are both necessary elements to prove in each kind of an unlawful detainer,[87] except for those not requiring notice at all.[88] Just like the lease agreement becomes the "Exhibit 1," the notice will be the "Exhibit 2" of the eviction complaint,[89] accompanied in most cases with a proof of service as the "Exhibit 3.[90]" More on the service of notice below.

TYPES OF THE NOTICE

Since the eviction notice may be based on different grounds, different types of notices exist. Commonly the type of the notice is announced in the notice's header. Identifying the type of the notice is paramount to notice validity, because different kinds invoke different requirements, different necessary disclosures, and varying procedural steps.

Most common notice denominations are:

- "notice to pay or quit" for a non-payment of rent, a curable kind of notice, or one "framed in the alternative.[91]" This notice tells its recipient that, if the problem is "cured" by paying the rent, the tenant needs not to "quit" or vacate the property;

- "notice to cure of quit" for a violation of a term, other than payment of rent, also a curable kind of notice, framed in the alternative;

A. Volkov. Eviction Notice In San Francisco.

- "notice to quit" for a violation of a term, other than payment of rent, when such violation is not curable or the demand of cure is not required; a non-curable kind of notice;

- "notice of termination of tenancy," another non-curable kind of notice, used for terminating tenancies when no violation or breach occurred. This type of notice is also used when a violation of a term, other than payment of rent, is defined to require this kind of notice.

The purpose of the eviction notice is to inform tenants that their tenancy is terminated, or in certain time and under certain conditions will be terminated. The eviction notice does not change the terms of the tenancy and should not be confused with the notice given under CC § 827.[92]

I. COMMONLY REQUIRED NOTICE ELEMENTS

A. Property Description

Sufficient definition of a real property, possession of which is being recovered, is a material term of the lease agreement and the notice. "The statute requires that the notice include a demand for the "property," and therefore it would seem to follow logically that the "property" must be described." Cal. Real Estate Law & Practice, Ch.7, ¶210.21 (Mathew Bender) cites *King v. Connolly*.[93]

The standard proposed in *King v. Connolly* is that the notice is sufficient if it "indicated with reasonable certainty, and to a certainty easily intelligible to the defendant, that the premises now sued for were the premises therein demanded of him." *Id*. at 238-239.

King v. Connolly is a San Francisco case, albeit 142 years old. Rental practice in the city became more nuanced since then on the subject of property description. For instance, if recovery of possession is sought for a portion of a real property without an independent "alienable" title, such an "in law" apartment, or a portion of premises occupied by a roommate tenant under an independently handled tenancy, the description of the property may need to be more specific than giving a general postal address. This is because, under the Rent Ordinance, single-family residencies are more often than not considered and treated as multi-family units.[94]

B. Parties

Relevant parties must be identified. For the non-fault evictions, identity of the issuers and recipients of the notice is a material element and deserves its own discussion in Chapter III, sub-sections V and X. And for all notices regardless of the type, it is important to identify the target recipients, occupants of the property. This is not as simple as just naming the tenants listed on the lease. The notice must aim at covering all occupants of the property, so that someone who is left out cannot later claim being not served with the notice.

The general rule is that "[s]ervice on tenant of notice to quit is notice to his cotenants,[95]" but any opportunity for creating a later argument of not receiving notice should be avoided. Caution must be exercised in naming occupants not previously acknowledged by the landlord. Naming those in the notice may create an implication of accepting them as valid subtenants, an unnecessary complication.

If there is any doubt about liability of the parties (not shown on the face of the lease, or the lease is oral, or some of the parties were not parties to the lease), it worth noting that the liability of co-occupants is presumed to be joint and several.[96]

My preferred language is this:

> To: JOHN DOE, JANE DOE, tenants in possession, BOB DOE, and all other tenants, subtenants, and occupants in a form of tenancy unknown, collectively referred to as "YOU," claiming to have a right to possess the premises located at: [followed by a property description]

John and Jane Doe would be the persons named under the lease or its subsequent amendments, Bob Doe would be the person known by name and known to occupy the property [if previously acknowledged by the landlord], and the remaining part would cover the occupants unknown.

There is a San Francisco-specific caveat in naming parties in the notice: Rules 6.14, 6.15A, 6.15B, 6.15D, and 6.15E.[97] The problem is in acknowledging previously unacknowledged co-occupants. A notice stated "in alternative" can be cured, and even a notice framed as a final and ultimate termination can later be rescinded, or the eviction following those notices either never commences, or settles, or loses in court. In theory, after any of those events the parties get back to square one, yet the notice will remain a written document evidencing affirmative acknowledgment of some additional co-occupants. Those so acknowledged may then gain status of co-tenants under the lease, at par with the original or "master" tenants or previously approved subtenants.

The danger of acknowledging lateral co- and sub-occupants is exposed in many publications, including in-detail coverage in several articles published by the San Francisco Apartment Association.[98] I, too, had a chance to write about the issue's procedural angle in 2013.[99] With the recent Ordinance 171- 15, rules regarding subtenants have changed, and the kinds and types of allowed co-occupancy were expanded. However, an *unauthorized* occupant, unless deemed approved, is still not allowed to reside at the property.

This issue can be addressed by expressly stating in the notice that, for any persons other than those named on the lease or previously and separate authorized by the landlord, the notice shall not be deemed as acceptance or authorization of any individuals mentioned in this notice as approved co-tenants, subtenants, or in any way or form authorized residents of the subject property.

In any scenario, the call shall be for including in the notice as many known persons who claim possession, as possible. In the eviction context it is more beneficial to name all known persons in the notice and in the consequent complaint. When acknowledged and named in the papers, these persons can be properly dealt with through the eviction process. Keep in mind that those whose names are skipped can still appear in the consequent eviction lawsuit by laying a prejudgment claim for possession.[100]

Attention shall be also paid as to how the enforcing party is identified on the notice. In some types of notices, contact information of the landlord is required by statute to be included in the notice,[101] in some types of termination disclosures had to be made prior to issuance of the notice, such as when there was a sale or a change of in the information related to payment of rent.[102] Also when the termination follows change of title due to a foreclosure, perfection of title is required prior to issuance of the eviction notice.[103]

C. Grounds For Termination

"[A] landlord may normally evict a tenant for any reason or for no reason at all, but he may not evict for an improper reason.[104]" Since the recovery of possession via unlawful detainer is a remedy strictly statutory in character, statement of the grounds upon which that recovery is sought is required.[105] The grounds have to exist at the time of eviction trial,[106] and made known in the notice.[107]

In the State of California, there are cases when the landlord needs no particular reason to terminate a tenancy. Such is the termination of a "periodic" tenancy, *i.e.* a tenancy running in defined term cycles, usually month-to-month, until terminated by a notice.[108] Not so in San Francisco.

In San Francisco, each eviction requiring a notice is subject to the Rent Ordinance.[109] Even evictions under CC §§ 1946, 1946.1, fall under coverage of the Rent Ordinance[110] and thus will require a "just cause,[111]" which shall be identified in the notice. There is a narrow exception of the general rule,[112] and those evictions are administered under the statewide law, they may thus require no grounds for the notice, or even no notice at all.

Particular grounds and elements of an eviction notice vary significantly, based on the corresponding applicable cause. They are reviewed further in this book, on per-cause basis.

D. Expiration Of The Notice

Notice is always definite in time, since it commands the tenant to do, or not to do, a certain act before the notice's expiration. It has to be unequivocal.[127] Non-compliance with the notice entitles a landlord to file an unlawful detainer—a tenant's failure to comply is measured at the expiration of the time period set in the notice.[113]

It is no coincidence that, in the description of what constitutes tenant's failure to comply, there is a statement of when the notice expires.[114] A landlord will not prevail on a prematurely filed complaint.[115]

Statutes only define minimally required time periods. A notice required to give a tenant three days may allow for a longer time period.[116] A lease agreement may also require a longer time than the one set in statutes.[117] Also important is to observe any required extension of time, such as 180 days under CC § 1942.5(a),[118] if there were elements for a potential argument of retaliation.

E. Contact Information

Contact information is expressly required in some and implied in some other eviction notices.[119] It also comes handful in the next stage of eviction, when a landlord has to prove the non-compliance with the notice's demand—it can be established through the witness mentioned as a person of contact on the notice. Also, since the notices contain a provision for the "to quit" part of the demand, possession of the property has to be "delivered up" and someone on the landlord's side has to be contacted for that reason. Procedures for retrieving or abandoning tenant's personal property and dealing with the security deposit further support the idea of specifying contact information in the notice.

F. Statement Of Good Faith

Not every eviction notice needs for its validity a statement that the possession is sought in good faith, although for eviction under some grounds acting in good faith is expressly required.[120] The landlord is still obligated to act in good faith in each and every case of eviction,[121] such as that "the landlord's dominant motive for recovering possession" is not some other reason, but a cause enumerated under the Rent Ordinance.[122] However, a mere issuance and service of the eviction notice does not indicate bad faith or duress.[123]

Since November 9, 2015, amendment of Sec. 37.9(c), the landlord now has to "plead and prove" that at least one of the enumerated "just causes" was the "the dominant motive for recovering possession."

Absence of good faith or a permissible dominant motive is a defense to eviction, including a defense of retaliation.[124] A counter-argument may be made that the retaliation defense statute requires that the tenant acts in good faith.[125]

Landlords acting in good faith are statutorily protected from imposition of rent stabilization program fines and penalties.[126] It can be said that by CC § 1947.7 good faith is presumed when the landlord substantially complies with the ordinance, but the substantial compliance is not clearly written in this statute and appears to be defined in circular reasoning, through acting in good faith.

If your notice is issued in good faith, you may opt to state so on the face of the notice; and in any case, avoid issuing notices lacking good faith altogether.

G. Statement Whether This Notice Supersedes Other Notices

The notice has to be unequivocal and unambiguous. "The landlord must use language upon which the tenant can safely act.[127]" The landlord may issue several notices,[128] either simultaneously or subsequently,[129] or a notice stating several grounds,[130] although it is important to know, on what particular notice or ground the eviction action is later based.[131]

An explanation of what notices are still in effect will assist the recipient in understanding of the currently pending demands and provide clarity of the landlord's position, thus eliminating a tenant's potential argument of an ineffective notice due to the notice's vagueness.

Imagine if a 3-day notice to Pay or Quit was issued together with a terminating 60-day notice.[132] By mere difference in time periods, there can be several chances for a tenant to fail to pay, or to violate another covenant warranting an issuance of a 3-day notice against him, while remaining in possession under the longer termination notice. If in this hypothetical the tenant will fail to pay for a second time, a new 3-day notice to pay or quit will indicate that it does supersede prior "pay or quit" notice but does not supersede the still-pending 60-day termination notice.

For the similar reasons, the notice shall either be consistent with the terms of the lease, or expressly state that, if default is cured, the notice does not alternate the terms of the lease. This precaution is due to the amended in 2011 Rule 12.20, which prohibits eviction for unilateral changes of the lease terms (except for terms otherwise authorized, see discussion in *Kardosh*[133]), and to that extent limits amendment of leases otherwise available under CC § 827.

H. Date And Signature

There is no unified opinion among authorities regarding signing and dating an eviction notice. CEB California Landlord-Tenant Practice (04/2014) §8.90 says signature is required, and cites although an unpublished, but a very instructive case in support. CEB Cal. Eviction Defense Manual (06/2014), §6.13, and Cal. Real Estate Law & Practice, Ch.7, ¶210.21 (Mathew Bender), both cite *Cavanaugh v. High*,[134] as an example of authority where signing and dating were found unnecessary.

A. Volkov. Eviction Notice In San Francisco.

CCP § 1161 does not mention a requirement of signing or dating of the notice. However, the holding in *Cavanaugh* was based on two facts: the notice was personally served, and that service was acknowledged. These two facts effectively established both the date and the person of that service of notice. In practice, notices are more often posted and mailed than personally served, and service is not always acknowledged by the recipients.

A case cited in Cal. Evict. Defense Manual, *supra, Earl Orchard Co. v. Fava,*[135] also comments on evidentiary importance of authority of notice issuers, and on establishing the date of termination of tenancy, both facts in which signing and dating the notice may assist.

It was held sufficient if an attorney sings a notice for his clients.[136] Court in *Earl Orchard* also held that signing a notice by the landlord's agent is sufficient.

There is also a discussion about sufficiency of authority to sign a notice by one landlord if other co-owners or cosigning lessors exist. Validity of a particular notice signed by lesser than all co-owners or their agents will depend on the facts. It was held generally acceptable for one tenant-in-common to evict from the entire property.[137] It was also held curable if co-owners later join or ratify the noticing party in the action.[138] Some types of eviction causes contain express requirements on co-ownership, *e.g.*, at least 25% of ownership for an "owner move-in" eviction.[139]

If still unsure about signing and dating, analyze the need from the perspective of later proving the fact of service and the date of termination of tenancy at trial. A signed notice may[140] provide you with an additional witness to prove genuineness of the writing[141] (the notice). A date gives you at least a presumption of when the notice was served.

Some authority refers to signing as a "safe practice,[142]" and I agree. Yet, there is no indication that a notice will be defective, if it lacks either of these two elements, provided that the fact of service, the date of service, and the fact of all co-owners' assent, can all be proved at trial.

I. Information About The Rent Board

Prior to November 9, 2015, landlords were required to inform the readers of their eviction notices that the advice regarding the notice is available from the Rent Board. Back then, there was a discussion among practitioners of how detailed the disclosure has to be, and with what variations in language and timing or service landlords can safely get away with.

This discussion is no more, and the current requirement is quite simple. There is a multilingual form (Form 1007) published by the Rent Board, and "[a] landlord shall attach a copy of the form that is in the primary language of the tenant to a notice to vacate before serving the notice, except that if the tenant's primary language is not English, Chinese, Spanish, Vietnamese, Tagalog or Russian, the landlord shall attach a copy of the form that is in English to the notice.[143]"

If it is unclear for a particular eviction, whether it falls within the jurisdiction of the Rent Board, Form 1007 can still be attached, just in case. You may disclaim that the subject tenancy does not seem to be regulated by the Rent Ordinance notwithstanding the attached form, and further include a qualifier similar to this: "advice regarding this notice, *and whether it is regulated by the Residential Rent Stabilization and Arbitration Board*, is available from the Residential Rent Stabilization and Arbitration Board of the City and County of San Francisco, 25 Van Ness Avenue, Suite No. 320, San Francisco, CA 94102-6033."

J. Notice Of Abandoning Personal Property

Often when a tenant vacates, items of tenant's personal property remain left behind. It will simplify the eviction if the left items can be deemed abandoned and dealt with expeditiously. Effective January 1, 2013, CC § 1946 and § 1946.1 were updated, among other statutes,[144] to demand inclusion in the notices, "in substantially the same form," the following language:

> "State law permits former tenants to reclaim abandoned personal property left at the former address of the tenant, subject to certain conditions. You may or may not be able to reclaim property without incurring additional costs, depending on the cost of storing the property and the length of time before it is reclaimed. In general, these costs will be lower the sooner you contact your former landlord after being notified that property belonging to you was left behind after you moved out."

This is the requirement expressly stated in CC §§ 1946, 1946.1, but nothing prevents a landlord from including the same clause in all other notices, in order to streamline dealing with the left behind personal property of a vacated tenant.

K. Notice About Tenant's Option To Request Initial Inspection.

CC § 1950.5(f)(1) grants a tenant with a right to request an initial inspection of the property and the landlord (as the party terminating the tenancy) shall inform the tenant about this right in writing. This is applicable to all eviction notices except the ones done pursuant to CCP §1161. While informing the tenant can be done separately, it may just as well be included in the notice.

L. Notice Of Debtor's Rights

An eviction notice may be deemed a debt collection attempt.[145] It is more obvious when the notice demands unpaid rent, but it can be argued in situations when the notice is issued on other grounds, and still indirectly asks of recovery of debt in some form. An argument stems from the fact that any eviction may involve accounting for or against the tenant's security deposit. Landlord's holding of the tenants' security deposit creates a creditor-debtor relationship.[146]

When landlords collect for themselves, they might be excluded from *some*[147] of the requirements, but when an agent is involved even that exemption may no longer apply. Attorneys should be particularly cautious in the light of the Supreme Court decision in *Jerman v. Carlisle,*[148] a harsh holding against attorney-agents of a debt collector.

CEB Cal. Eviction Defense Manual cites *De Dios v. International Realty & RC Invs.* (9th Cir., 2011) 641 F.3d 1071, where it was held that the property manager signing the notice for a landlord is not a debt collector within the Federal Debt Collection Practices Act. The reasoning in *De Dios* is based on the fact that the manager had obtained a right to collect from tenants before any default or debt occurred, and on that ground exempt from the definition of a debt collector. I assume the same line or reasoning may apply to an attorney who got engaged to represent a landlord before that particular default occurred, but I prefer to avoid this argument altogether by including the requisite disclaimers in the notice, addressing the Fair Debt Collection Practices Act, 15 USCS § 1692 *et seq.*, and the California Rosenthal Act, Civ. Code § 1788, *et seq.*

M. Notice In Other Languages

Since the general principle for an eviction notice is to be unequivocally clear about its demands, an occupant of the property not speaking English needs a notice in a language that occupant understands.

Since November 9, 2015, Ordinance update, all eviction notices given under Section 37.9 are required to include Form 1007,[149] informing the tenant in several languages that advice about the notice is provided by the Rent Board. (Sec. 37.9(c)).

And even prior to 2015 update, certain residential notices were already statutorily required to be given in five languages. Such is the case with the foreclosure sale,[150] nuisance behavior involving unlawful weapons,[151] or possession of controlled substance.[152]

For notices not subject to the statutes cited above, the decision to issue it in any other language is one for the landlord. Before the notice drafter should run to an interpreter, an important first step is to review the underlying lease agreement, to see in what language it was negotiated.

Note that for the parties who primarily deal in a foreign language, the translation requirement exists since 1976, and it expressly includes leases.[153] The requirement for subsequent notices would be determined based on whether the lease was negotiated in English or another language. The rule of thumb is: the notice should match the language of the lease. Since the notice is also served on unknown occupants, an English version of the notice shall always be included, as well as the Form 1007.

N. Additional Requirements For Government Subsidized Tenancies.

Tenancies existing under the "Section 8" and other government-subsidy programs may impose additional requirements on the notices issued to terminate those tenancies. Most notably, it may affect the time length of the eviction notice.[154] Whenever possible, this book mentions applicable elements, corresponding to the types of notices discussed. In general, "the notice requirements of this [S.F. Admin. Code] Section 37.9 shall be required in addition to any notice required as part of the tenant-based rental assistance program.[155]"

O. Anything else?

The holding in San Francisco case *Naylor v. Super. Ct.*[156] provides some guidance on what may or should be included. A copy of an applicable ordinance section attached to the notice was held to suffice for proper disclosures otherwise omitted in the notice. (*Id*. at 7-8). The court in *Naylor* declined to "read-in" any additional hypothetical conditions for the notice and observed that "[w]hile the notice provisions must be strictly complied with, the courts are not required to stretch their language to include a notice provision not expressly stated." (*Id*.) An earlier case of an SFHA eviction also held that it is "unnecessary to attach grievance procedure to complaint.[157]"

SERVICE OF NOTICE

This section contains only few basic commentaries on the service of notice, ones I consider important for perfecting and proving the service particularly in San Francisco. More guidance on the service of notice is covered in statewide landlord-tenant treatises.

Service of an eviction notice issued under CCP §§ 1161, 1161a, 1161b has to be made in compliance with CCP § 1162. Service of a 30/60 day termination notice issued under CC §§ 1946, 1946.1 may also be done per CCP § 1162, as well as via registered or certified mail.[158] While service under CCP § 1162 does not extend the time for the notice's term when the notice is mailed,[159] there is no known authority instructing whether such extension is not added when the notice is mailed only.[160]

Unlike service of process of summons, which requires leave of court to serve by posting and mailing,[161] an eviction notice may be served by posting the notice on the premises and mailing its copy to the last known address of the tenant.[162]

Service of notice is also different from service of summons, because individual service of all co-tenants is not required; service on one tenant is sufficient service on all co-tenants.[163] At the same time, effort has to be made to include in the notice all known occupants, including sub-tenants, so that the service of notice is effective on them.[164] Inclusion of subtenants and other occupants has to be done with caution, as discussed in Section ¶ I(B) (Parties) of the Commonly Required Notice Elements, above.

The notice can be served by the landlords themselves or by their authorized agents.[165] However, landlords should always consider hiring a licensed servicer of process, because proper service of notice is a material element[166] to prove later in court,[167] and having a third-party witness to testify in support of the proper service is beneficial. In case of the proof signed by a licensed server, there may be no need to testify, since the proof is presumed valid, under Evid. Code § 647.[168] For all practical matters, notices served with the checks, such as an owner-move-in notices, shall be handled with additional care. Unless the tenants can be served in person, I prefer to have the actual checks mailed via registered mail, while including only a copy of the checks with the notices posted and mailed via regular mail.

Make several copies of the notice. At least two of them will be served on the tenant (one for a tenant and one for all unknown occupants), one goes for your file, and one has to be filed with the Rent Board[169] within 10 days of service together with its proof of service, for all types of notices except a 3-day notice for non-payment of rent.[170] It is advised, and under some eviction causes required, to file the proof of service together with the notice.[171]

The Rent Board "make[s] no determination as to the legal sufficiency of notices to vacate filed pursuant to Ordinance Section 37.9(c) or of procedures followed by the parties.[172]" Notices terminating government-subsidized housing shall be sent to agency administering the program.[173] For instance, copies of the notices related to the San Francisco "Section 8[174]" program are given to the San Francisco Housing Authority[175] ("SFHA").

Three comments on the 10-day filing requirement with the Rent Board:

(1) It only exempts the "*three*-day notices to vacate or pay rent." If your notice provides for any more number of days, file a copy with the Rent Board.

(2) As discussed above, in some situations evictions are exempt from the Rent Board jurisdiction, yet it might be unclear if the exemption applies, or it might be a partial exemption. When in doubt—consult an attorney whether to file it anyway, because a filed notice creates a mark on the property's "record" in the Board's database, raising a potential question from a reviewing party in the future (a buyer, a city department, or court), and if such filing was unnecessary, marking the record is similarly better to be avoided.

(3) You may have noticed that Section 37.9(c), fifth sentence, while requiring a copy of the notice to be filed within 10 days, does not expressly demand that it is the *landlord* who has to file it. Unlike the instructions in sentences surrounding the filing requirement, where it directly says who has to do what ("A landlord shall ..." [preceding sentence]; "The District Attorney shall ..." [following sentence]), filing of the notice just has to be done. Indeed, it is often the case in my experience that it is the *recipient* of the notice, the tenant, who files a petition for wrongful eviction with the Rent Board, also files a copy of the notice as the petition's exhibit and does so within the required 10 days. The advice is simple: landlords

should cause copies of their notices be filed with the Rent Board within 10 days, while tenants should avoid filing a copy of the notice during the same time.

To count correctly when the notice expires, do not include the day it was served on and, if the last day to perform falls on a weekend or holiday, include the first following business day.[176] This rule makes service of a 3-day notice on Wednesday, Thursday, or Friday all be counted as served on Friday. If Monday is a holiday, then a 3-day notice served on Wednesday will expire on the next Tuesday, effectively on the same day as if it were served on Saturday,[177] three days later. Note that under the 2019 amendment of CCP § 1161, effective September 1, 2019, "Saturdays and Sundays and other judicial holidays" are excluded from the 3-day count for the notices brought under 1161(2) and 1161(3) grounds.

At the same time, keep in mind that delaying the service of a notice for too long may invalidate the notice if it becomes inaccurate. Imagine a situation with a pay-or-quit demand for rent, in which, during the time allowed for tenant's performance, another month starts with a new rent due, while the tenant pays the old sum demanded in the notice. This is what happened in the *Kruger v. Reyes*[178] case and the notice was held invalid. In the case involving a non-fault eviction notice, the court observed that "suspicious timing of the eviction notice will be considered evidence of bad faith.[179]"

Note that no additional extension of time for service by mail under CCP § 1013 applies to the service of notice.[180] There is a more recent (1990) authority holding that the "service of the three-day notice by posting and mailing is effective on the date the notice is posted and mailed.[181]" But see an older 1982 case allowing to extend time for a mailed copy of the notice.[182]

NOTICE ELEMENTS FOR PARTICULAR JUST CAUSES

All evictions can be divided in two types: ones based on an act or a failure to act by the evictee, called "for fault" evictions, and those typically triggered by circumstances outside of the evictee's control, often called "non-fault" evictions. San Francisco Rent Ordinance lists all "just causes" (allowed grounds to commence the eviction) in one chapter,[183] starting the list with the for-fault causes. This book follows the Ordinance order for convenience of reference, where the notices similarly grouped by "for-fault" and "no fault" evictions. Materials listed

A. Volkov. Eviction Notice In San Francisco.

before were generally applicable to notices of both kinds. The following section covers the "for-fault" notices (section II), and the "no fault" notices to be covered in section III. The following section covers the "for-fault" notices (section II), and the "no fault" notices to be covered in section III. Current publication includes general elements and the first four non-fault grounds for eviction: owner move-in, relative move-in, recovery of possession for sale following a condo-conversion and termination due to demolition or permanent removal of the unit from the housing use.

II. FOR FAULT EVICTIONS

1. Non-payment of rent. SFRO § 37.9(a)(1)(A).

(a) Type and length of the notice: 3-Day To Pay Or Quit.

An action for "non payment of rent" is evicting a tenant who failed to pay rent when it was due. It is allowed by the Rent Ordinance.[184] The eviction notice under this cause is the only notice of which copy is *not* required to be filed with the Rent Board,[185] if it is a 3-day notice.

This notice is a "notice to pay or quit," a curable kind (one "framed in the alternative[186]"), allowing a tenant to save the tenancy from for-feiture if the problem is "cured" by paying the rent as instructed. See also, Civ. Code § 3275, on relief from forfeiture.

The statute expressly allows demanding from tenants to cure their non-payment in three days.[187] The demand can be made only after the rent became due.[188] The 3-day period may not be shortened, but it must be extended to "exclud[e] Saturdays and Sundays and other judicial holi-days,"[189] or if there is an agreement between the parties,[190] and it may also be extended by the landlord's own choice. Extending time of the notice may trigger necessity to file its copy with the Rent Board—as mentioned earlier, only issuance of the three day notice for non-payment is express-ly excluded from filing a copy of such notice with the Rent Board.

When the rent is "due" is not always obvious. <u>First</u>, the written lease, if one exists, has to be closely examined: for when the due date is set (not always written as the first day of the month and sometimes entirely omitted), whether the rent is required be paid "in advance[191]" of that date, whether there is a grace period, and, if yes, whether that grace period is defined as extending the due date or not. In absence of express terms, the statute in California provides for the payment may sometime be due at the end of the paid-for term.[192] <u>Second</u>, analyze the prior conduct between the parties, what due dates or periods were in practice. Said conduct may be held controlling over the express terms of the lease, especially with regard to the grace period.[193] While *Miller & Starr* does not cite a case directly addressing the issue of a grace period in leases affecting landlord's ability to evict prior to the expiration of the grace period, the treatise refers to a holding arising from a debtor's dues under a note, saying that a late payment under the note does not justify foreclosure.[194]

The rent payment must be made within the time specified, with one notable exception stated in CCP § 1161(2): if the notice does not provide for an address allowing "personal delivery" of the payment, "then it shall be conclusively presumed that upon the mailing of any rent or notice to the owner by the tenant to the name and address provided, the notice or rent is deemed received by the owner **on the date posted**, if the tenant can show proof of mailing to the name and address provided by the owner." Accord, CC § 1962(f).

Your notice therefore would be more efficient, if it provides for personal delivery of the payment; otherwise the landlord should wait additional time to see if the payment posted within the noticed three days failed to arrive in mail a few days later.

As a side comment, there are cases distinguishing between the tenant's effected payment (such as cash or a direct bank deposit) and the *offer* to make a payment (payment by a personal check). Such are the recent decisions in *Kruger v. Reyes* (2014) and *Bawa v. Terhune* (2019).[195] A decision issued a few months prior to *Kruger* did not make this distinction and held a payment tendered in check as paid.[196] However, that court had ruled based on a different set of facts: the notice there was already admitting a payment of a previous month's rent (demanding only a half of the next month's rent), while the unlaw-ful detainer complaint alleged the whole sum as still due.

(b) Stated Amount: less is Ok, more is not Ok.

A three-day notice may include up to one-year worth of owed back rent, and no more.[197] The amount of rent due must be stated in the Pay or Quit eviction notice, and it must be accurate. "A notice that seeks rent in excess of the amount due is invalid and will not support an unlawful detainer action.[198]" This rule led in 2016 *North 7th Street* case to an outcome that no rent was deemed collectable from an in-law unit, as the rental agreement held void and unenforceable.[199]

Significantly overstating the amount due is fatal for the notice.[200] Over-stating the amount just a little had also been ruled as a reason to inva-lidate the notice,[201] although at least one court called such increases a *"de minimis"* overstatement and a "trifling error.[202]" The difference between the two cases cited for this rule is that one lease operated under the rent ordinance, while the other had not. Thus, for our purposes of exploring what would be a valid notice in San Francisco, there should be no overstatement of the due rent.

The *"de minimis"* doctrine also applies to analyzing tenant's performance in tendering the payment to satisfy the notice and obligation to pay rent. "[W]hen a landlord refuses to accept rent that is one penny short of the required amount, without any legitimate intent other than to manufacture a default in order to evict a tenant, a tenant may assert the landlord's bad faith as an unlawful detainer defense."[203]

Whether the demanded rent amount is what is really "due," depends on rent increases made prior to the issuance of the notice. For not rent-controlled residential properties, compliance with CC § 827 is required. For rent-controlled properties, additional conditions and limitations on the rent increase are added by S.F. Admin. Code, Sections 37.3, 37.8.

There is also a San Francisco trial court decision sustaining demurrer to a notice for its inclusion of the late fees in the total amount due.[204] Demurrer was based on the case holding that an unlawful detainer for non-payment of rent should not be for any money but the rent arrears.[205] There is a 2018 decision from a non-rent-controlled Humboldt county, finding a notice invalid for including $50 late fee, on the grounds of it being improper liquidated damages.[206]

For these reasons, inclusion of the late fees or other coincidental fees in the notice should be avoided.

Notice drafters thus should avoid the risk of overstating the amount due, leaning to err on the side of understatement. *Under*stating the amount is acceptable.[207]

(c) Where, how, and to whom to pay.

Tenant's knowledge of where and whom to pay may affect timing of the rent payment and even invoke the "mailbox" rule in determining when the payment was made, such as to deem it made when posted.[208]

Non-payment eviction notices are often attacked for non-compliance with the statutory required descriptions for the manner of payment. This includes "strict compliance" with the disclosure requirements for a subsequent owner per CC § 1962, as a prerequisite to evicting for non-payment of rent.[209] San Francisco local regulations have similar provisions as part of the eviction-control ordinance, including ones for the new owners through purchase and by way of foreclosure.[210]

A. Volkov. Eviction Notice In San Francisco.

The required elements for the notice are all listed in the statute, CCP § 1161. I formatted the relevant portion of the section to be easier to read, emphasizing the conjunctive and disjunctive parts:

> "notice, in writing, ... stating ... the name, telephone number, and address of the person to whom the rent payment shall be made,
> **and**, if payment may be made personally, the usual days and hours that person will be available to receive the payment (provided that, if the address does not allow for personal delivery, then it shall be conclusively presumed that upon the mailing of any rent or notice to the owner by the tenant to the name and address provided, ...),
> **or** the number of an account in a financial institution into which the rental payment may be made, and the name and street address of the institution (provided that the institution is located within five miles of the rental property),
> **or** if an electronic funds transfer procedure has been previously established, that payment may be made pursuant to that procedure, or possession of the property..."

A lot of notices failed for having just some but not all of the required information, most often missing the telephone number, name, or address "of the person to whom the rent payment shall be made," especially the telephone number.

From the commencement of the lease, landlords should consider carefully all cons and pros before establishing a policy for payments of rent by any "electronic funds transfer procedure." It is procedurally easier to deal with tenancies where no electronic payment policy was established.

In the notice, landlords desiring to avoid arguments over electronic payments and direct deposits, shall provide tenants with a way to make a payment personally. There is a case law developed for the situations when the methods of payments stated in the notice differ from the customary practice developed between the parties under the lease. Notice language under CCP § 1161 is held controlling in the eviction proceedings.[211]

(d) Statement of landlord's election of forfeiture.

The notice shall include a statement informing the recipient that the landlord elects to declare forfeiture of the lease. Without that statement in the notice, a tenant may challenge that the judgment may not forfeit the lease.[212]

If you are already facing a situation where the express election of forfeiture was not included, an argument can be made that the notice was sufficient if there was an unequivocal statement "that would indicate an intention on the part of the landlord to terminate the lease by forfeiture, or to insist on a right to reenter, if the rent be not paid.[213]"

(e) Other required elements.

Other elements covered in the "Commonly Required Notice Elements" section of this book apply, such as: property description [¶ I(A)], parties [¶ I(B)], date and signature [¶ I(H)], information about the Rent Board [¶ I(I)], notice of abandoning personal property [¶ I(J)], notice of debtor's rights [¶ I(L)], notice given in other languages [¶ I(M)], optionally including a statement, whether this notice supersedes other notices [¶ I(G)]. Notice of an option to request initial inspection does not apply here.

(f) Section 8 application.

The same 3-day notice in compliance with CCP § 1161(2) must be given in terminating a tenancy for non-payment of rent under the "Section 8" subsidy program.[214]

Termination of the government-subsidized tenancy has its own additional requirements, including a requirement of service of the copy of the notice on the sponsoring/subsidizing agency. There are, in fact, several different housing-subsidy programs all collectively referred to as "Section 8." While each has its own slightly varying requirements, they all acknowledge a right for landlord to evict for non-payment of rent.[215]

(g) An issue of waiver or equitable estoppel.

If an issue of waiver or equitable estoppel is contemplated, the notice shall have the language addressing it and notifying the tenant about no waiver by the landlord. Landlord's waiver nullifies the notice and reinstates the lease, the same effect as what the tenant's cure of the noticed default achieves, if the default were curable.[216]

A common defense against this eviction notice is the argument of "waiver," where a tenant alleges that the landlord waived previously noticed fault by accepting rent after the notice was served. The general rule of waiver is known since times of Sir Edward Coke[217] and requires that a landlord accepts rent in "with full knowledge of all the facts" relevant to the breach.[218] "Waiver is an intentional relinquishment of a known right.[219]" If the lease contains an express "no waiver" clause, the landlord may argue that acceptance of rent did not result in waiver, especially if that was communicated to the tenants.[220] "While waiver is a question of intent, the cases have required some positive evidence of rejection on the landlord's part or a specific reservation of rights in the lease to overcome the presumption that tender and acceptance of rent creates.[221]" Notably, even acceptance of a portion of a rent, or an installment payment, may constitute a waiver.[222]

On the other hand, any illegal term or condition of the lease agreement is void and unenforceable, even if seems to be a waiver or a promise acknowledged by the party, and even if that party is a landlord.[223]

Some tenants in the situation of a "no waiver" clause argue a similar defense of equitable estoppel.[224] "The elements of the doctrine of estoppel ... are ... as follows: "Whenever a party has, by his . . . conduct, intentionally and deliberately led another to believe a particular thing true and to act upon such belief, he is not, in any litigation arising out of such . . . conduct, permitted to contradict it."" *Salton Community Srvcs.*, 256 Cal.App.2d, *Id.* at 533, citing Cal. Evid. Code § 623. The elements of estoppel making it similar to waiver are that the landlord must act "intentionally and deliberately" in leading the tenant to believe in a certain relief, and to act upon it. Therefore, if there are facts establishing non-existence of a waiver or estoppel, stating these facts in the notice will help to rebut tenants' argument to the contrary.

A portion of the rent payable to the landlord directly by the government subsidizing program (such as the Section 8) is not considered "rent[225]" and may be distinguished for the purposes of defining a waiver.

(h) Two express exceptions under the Rent Ordinance.

The Rent Ordinance exempts two scenarios, in which the landlord may not use the ground of non-payment of rent to evict the tenant.

The first ground extends the prohibition imposed on the residential hotel operators, it does not allow to evict a tenant for failing to pay a charge prohibited by S.F. Police Code, Section 919.1 (the described charge would be assessed "for any person to visit" a tenant).

The second ground exempts from evicting tenants failing to pay their portion of a capital improvement passthrough fee. This exemption is probably in desuetude now, because its application is limited, especially because of its time limits, such as "where the capital improvement pass-through petition was filed prior to August 10, 2001." I don't know if there are many current tenancies left under this exemption, but certainly some may remain.

(i) One implied exception under S.F. Police Code § 3304.

There is a local program called the "Season of Sharing" or "S.O.S.," where various organizations step into the shoes of defaulting tenants and offer to pay for them their rent dues. Whether the landlord is under an obligation to accept rent so offered would depend on several factors. One is to comply with S.F. Police Code Section 3304, prohibiting discrimination based on the source of income. Landlords should be aware that the prohibition is not absolute. There are exemptions, stated under § 3304(c)(1): provisions of this section do not apply where the "prospective" tenant shares the use of either a bathroom or kitchen facility with the owner, or "the structure contains less than three dwelling units."

In addition to the stated exemptions, it can also be argued that where the S.F. Police Code treats such sponsored rent paid by a non-tenant (the sponsoring organization) to a non-tenant, the landlord, as "income," it directly contradicts the statewide definition, which reads: "[f]or the purposes of this section, "source of income" means lawful, verifiable income paid directly to a tenant or paid to a representative of a tenant. For the purposes of this section, a landlord is not considered a representative of a tenant.[226]"

Similarly cautious should be landlords who rent under the "Section 8" and alike government subsidized programs, where necessity of having a co-paying person may be deemed an "accommodation.[227]"

(j) caution in handling "in law" units.

Defendants often bring up a *"in pari delicto"* defense when being evicted from a non-conforming or illegal unit, such as a widely used in San Francisco an "in law" unit in a single-family house. Landlords should be aware that there are cases, when the court, while allowing to recover possession, had ordered to pay a refund to the tenant. A recent 2016 decision in the case *North 7th Street Associates v. Constante*[228] led to a particularly harsh result for the evicting landlord, not even allowing to recover possession.

One of the counter-defenses available to a landlord is the proper disclosure of the rental unit status to the tenant.[229]

2. Late payment of rent. SFRO § 37.9(a)(1)(B).

(a) Type and length of the notice: 30 or 60-Day Notice of Termination of Tenancy.

This eviction cause seems to be a twin of the non-payment of rent, but this eviction is treated differently. Although technically it is a breach of the term of a lease agreement (the lease demanding that the rent is due and payable on a certain date, and the rent is paid on a later date), the San Francisco Superior Court ruled that the "30 or 60 day notice required. Civil Code Section 1946.[230]"

The notice is almost always a 60-day notice.[231] There are statewide exceptions when it is a 30-day notice, covered in CC § 1946.1. Only subsection (c) fully applies to the tenancies in San Francisco (for tenancies existing for less than a year). The second exception, under subsection (d), involves a sale of the real property, which is not a valid ground to evict under the Rent Ordinance.[232] Although not stated in the cause itself, the Rent Board's "Fact Sheet 4" suggests that the tenant had been warned "more than once or twice" that this late payment of rent "is not acceptable to the landlord." Therefore, there is a strong suggestion for a preliminary notice, one or two, informing the tenants that their tardiness in paying rent will not be tolerated.

For terminating tenancy with an undefined term, no consequent 3-day notice is required.[233] The termination takes place on the date the notice expires, not when it is issued.[234] The notice must be valid at the time it expires, not necessarily when it is issued.[235]

(b) Statement of grounds.

In order for the notice to be valid under the Rent Ordinance, there must exist a ground falling under one of the "just causes" of the Rent Ordinance. It follows that such ground shall be asserted on a face of the notice, in order for the notice to be unambiguous and to survive an attack for compliance with the ordinance.[236]

The ground for this notice is tenant's paying rent habitually late. "Habitual late payment of rent – this means more than once or twice and the tenant has been warned that this is not acceptable to the landlord.[237]" Therefore, for the sufficient statement of this ground the notice shall indicate instances of the late payments of rent.

A. Volkov. Eviction Notice In San Francisco.

When the rent payment is late? This is easy to determine in presence of a written lease agreement, defining when the rent is due. The usual clause will assert that the rent is due on the 1st day of the month and is late if not paid when due, even when there is a gross period of time to pay without incurring a late fee (typically five days).

If there is no written agreement, or the applicable terms are not defined, the rent is due at the end of the applicable period, typically a month.[238]

There is still one more item to check, whether the tenant was provided sufficient contact information for payment of rent, including an address allowing for personal delivery.[239] If not, than the rent may be not late if was timely "posted" (measuring by when the rent was mailed, not when received.[240] While these requirements do not affect the underlying obligation to pay rent,[241] it certainly may render a later-arrived payment as one timely made, depending on how the elements of CC § 1962 will reflect on the facts.

(c) There is no cure or a statement in the alternative.

Unlike CCP § 1161, there is no "cure" or a statement in the alternative required for a notice pursuant to CC § 1946.[242] This type of the notice simply informs its recipients that the tenancy is terminated (or rather not renewed) at the specified period of time. For habitually late payment of rent, San Francisco Rent Ordinance allows such termination if the elements of the applicable just cause are satisfied, namely that (a) the tenant was late more than once or twice, and that (b) the landlord had warned the tenant that such conduct is unacceptable.

(d) Landlord's contact information—optional, but preferred.

Unlike the above-analyzed notice for non-payment of rent, where the landlord's detailed contact information is expressly required to be part of the notice by statute (CCP § 1161(2)), notice under CC § 1946 does not contain this requirement. Technically, a CC § 1946 is valid without any contact information provided. But include anyway, in full detail.

There are valid reasons for doing so. Tenant's ignorance of landlord's contact information may become an obstacle in an eviction, or increase time for tenant's delivery of payments or notices.[243] It as well seems necessary for a tenant to know how to contact a landlord in the case of a CC §§ 1946, 1946.1 eviction, where a landlord (as a terminating party) must inform the tenant about the tenant's right to request an inspection of the property prior to vacating it,[244] and also inform the tenant about applicable rent payments coming due during the pendency of the notice. It follows that a tenant needs to have an option to contact a landlord for the inspection request and to know to whom make a rent payment.

(e) Statement of abandoning personal property.

Effective January 1, 2013, a statement regarding tenant's abandonment of personal property, optional in other situations, is expressly required for notices given under CC §§ 1946, 1946.1, as stated in the current version of the statute.

(f) Statement of landlord's election of forfeiture.

Since the tenancy is "terminated" at the moment specified in this notice, a statement of forfeiture is not required for a notice issued pursuant to CC § 1946. CCP § 1174(a) explains that "the judgment shall also declare the forfeiture of that lease or agreement *if the notice required by Section 1161* states the election of the landlord to declare the forfeiture thereof." The subject notice is not one required by Section 1161, therefore, the rule from CCP § 1174 (no forfeiture in judgment unless its election is stated in the notice) does not apply.[245] If this eviction requires a follow-up filing of an unlawful detainer, make sure the prayor seeks termination of the agreement, not forfeiture.[246]

The reason lies in principal difference between the two types of evictions. A notice under CCP § 1161 leads to a termination of an otherwise active lease contract, hence it requires forfeiture of that contract. If a tenant had neither cured nor vacated the property, the following eviction is a lawsuit in contract, and only the judgment for a prevailing landlord terminates that lease contract. Compare this with a notice under CC §§ 1946, 1946.1, where the contract is terminated at the time set in the notice, granting a landlord a right to entry after that lease contract's termination.[247] If a tenant had not yet vacated at the expiration date, the following eviction in this scenario is a lawsuit in tort. Two 2007 decisions[248] contain a detailed discussion on when an eviction is founded in tort and when in contract.

Generally speaking, it may be permissible to include a statement of forfeiture in the notice, yet the decision to include this statement must be made based on the facts of a particular case. Consider that if the eviction is based on such tenant's conduct, to which the landlord had previously assented, it might be no longer strictly enforced to support forfeiture of the lease.[249]

See also the conversation above, under the notice for non-payment of rent, for an additional argument if the notice is attacked for no forfeiture clause, and the issues of waiver and equitable estoppel.

(g) Other required elements.

Other elements covered in the "Commonly Required Notice Elements" section of this book may apply, such as: property description [¶ I(A)], parties [¶ I(B)], statement whether this notice supersedes other notices [¶ I(G)], date and signature [¶ I(H)], information about the Rent Board [¶ I(I)], notice of an option to request initial inspection [¶ I(K)], notice of debtor's rights [¶ I(L)], notice given in other languages [¶ I(M)].

A copy of the notice together with its proof of service has to be filed with the Rent Board, under Section 37.9(c).

(h) Section 8 application.

Tenant's paying rent late may be a sufficient ground for eviction under the Section 8 subsidized tenancy.[250] However, several additional requirements are observed, including compliance with the applicable federal procedure, such as 24 CFR 247.3, and a showing that tenant's "late payments adversely affected the projector its financial stability." (*Gersten Cos., Id.*)

(i) An issue of waiver or equitable estoppel.

Similarly to this issue analyzed for non-payment of rent [¶ II(1)], the same defense of waiver or equitable estoppel[224] may be raised in attacking a notice for paying rent habitually late. The issue is even more applicable here, since there is a requisite element of landlord warning the tenant that such conduct (paying rent late) is unacceptable. In absence of a non-waiver clause in the written agreement, such warning may become a challenge for landlord to prove.

(j) An issue with serving subtenants and other occupants.

Generally, a CC § 1946 notice is required to be served only on the tenants mentioned in the lease.[251] However, two considerations make it prudent to serve on other occupants in San Francisco: (1) in case some of those occupants had established their right to occupy under

Rules 6.14, 6.15A-E, and (2) in case it is one of those subtenants or co-occupants who was the reason for late payments.

3. Frequent payment with bad checks. SFRO § 37.9(a)(1)(C).

(a) Type and Length of the Notice: a possible combination of a 3-day notice to pay or quit and a 30/60-day termination notice.

When a tenant "[g]ives checks which are frequently returned because there are insufficient funds in the checking account,[252]" he may be evicted. This is essentially similar to tenant's failure to perform by paying rent on time, analyzed above. Thus, a 30/60-day notice pursuant to CC §§ 1946, 1946.1 will apply.

However, this ground is different from paying rent habitually late, in that the rent is still paid under the later, yet more likely remains unpaid under the former. When the rent is not paid, because a bad check was tendered, a basic 3-day notice for non-payment of rent is applicable.

Frequent payment by bad checks calls for serving a combination of two notices: a 3-day notice for the current non-payment, and a 30/60-day termination notice for the pattern of habitually / frequent payments with bad checks.

(b) Statement whether this notice supersedes other notices.

In the situation where two simultaneous notices will be served, the drafter has to make sure that each of the concurrently served notices does not cancel out the other one. Therefore, the notice of superseding other notices shall be adjusted to exclude the corresponding notice.

(c) How many times is frequent.

This will be left for a trial court to decide, how many instances of bad payment of rent is sufficiently "frequent" for this eviction cause to be commenced. Merriam-Webster dictionary associates "frequent" with "habitually" as one of its alternative meanings.[253] If so, a definition given to us by the Rent Board on what is "habitually" (more than once or twice), may apply.

(d) An issue with the waiver.

All previously discussed concerns regarding the waiver apply here (see, ¶ II(1)(g), *supra*), and there is another twist to consider when two simultaneous notices are issued. The difference in operation and length of the notices' terms demand different steps from a landlord: the 3-day notice for non-payment of rent becomes actionable if no rent is paid within its set three days, yet the 30/60-day termination notice is not affected by a consequent rent payment, and the tenants are expected to pay for the time they are still occupying the premises.

Therefore, the issue is resolved based on when the payment of rent is offered: if within the three days, the 3-day notice is cured, and only proceeding on the 30/60-day notice remains. If offered after the three days, a landlord has a choice: either to accept the rent, waive the 3-day notice, and to proceed on the 30/60-day notice, or to return the rent to the tenant, because the eviction proceedings based on the 3-day notice have already commenced.[254]

(e) Other required elements.

Other terms, clauses, and issues are similar to the notice for late payment of rent, see ¶ II(2)(g), *supra*. Notice of an option to request initial inspection may apply [¶ I(K)]. A copy of the notice together with its proof of service has to be filed with the Rent Board.

(f) Worth noting.

Drafting bad checks or checks with insufficient funds is a practice exposing for both civil[255] and criminal[256] liability.

4. Violation of a lawful obligation or covenant of a tenancy. SFRO § 37.9(a)(2).

(a) Type and Length of the Notice: 10-day notice to cure or quit for a violation related to subletting;[257] or 3-day notice to cure or quit, under CCP § 1161(3), for majority of the situations not related to subletting.[258] A notice given under this section may not be a 3-day notice to quit without a given opportunity to cure.[259]

As covered under the late-payment cause above, a distinction between an action in tort and an action in contract defines the applicable statute and, in turn, the type and length of the notice.[248] A violation of a covenant makes it an action in contract by definition, hence the 3-day notice comes under CCP § 1161. Majority of the cases under this cause would fall under subsection 3 of this statute, requiring a notice stated in the alternative, to cure or quit.

Commission of "waste upon the demised premises, contrary to the conditions or covenants of his or her lease" *would* lead to a non-alternative 3-day notice to quit under CCP § 1161(4), but Sec. 37.9(a)(2) expressly requires to give an opportunity to cure. And since the new edition of this Section also requires the violation to be substantial, it all but eliminates a scenario, where the ground to evict under 37.9(a)(2) would be waste.

To fall under this section, (i) the lease has to contain a clause deeming such waste a substantial violation, and (iii) the waste should not be resulting in "substantial damage" to the rental unit. This is a narrow scenario, but not entirely impossible.[260] More often, however, commission of waste is dealt with under the cause 37.9(a)(3).

Notice for subletting violations was statutory extended to a minimum of 10 days and to be given with an opportunity to cure.[257]

(b) Exemptions and the narrowed scope of instances applicable to this cause.

The subject cause for eviction is inapplicable in the following situations:

> (i) Under CCP § 1161(3), this eviction is for "a neglect or failure to perform *other* conditions or covenants of the lease or agreement under which the property is held ... *than* the one for the payment of rent." Thus the violations related to payment of rent don't

belong here, but are dealt with under 37.9(a)(1), above, (the non-payment, late payment, and bad payment of rent).

(ii) Section 37.9(a)(2) excludes evictions for "an obligation to pay a charge prohibited by Police Code Section 919.1." S.F. Police Code § 919.1 prohibits operators, employees, and agents of a Residential Hotel[261] to "impose or collect a charge for any person to visit a guest or occupant of the hotel."

The S.F. Rent Ordinance also narrows application of CCP § 1161(3) in instances of subletting. Where the statute expressly applies to "a neglect or failure to perform other conditions or covenants of the lease or agreement under which the property is held, including any covenant not to assign or sublet," the Rent Ordinance defines, what kind of subletting is not actionable:

(iii) When the landlord had unreasonably withheld consent to a tenant to sublet for a "one-for-one replacement of the departing tenant(s).[262]" More details on this limitation are disclosed in the Rules 6.15B, 6.15D, and 6.15E. Note that this exemption does not bar all evictions for subletting, only ones where "the landlord has unreasonably withheld the right to sublet following a written request by the tenant." Sec. 37.9(a)(2)(A). Landlord's approval is deemed rendered if "If the landlord fails to respond to the tenant in writing with a description of the reasons for the denial of the request within 14 days of receipt of the tenant's written request." *Id.*

(iv) When tenants add relatives, provided they do so in compliance with rule 6.15D, so long as the total number does not exceed either the "maximum number permitted in the unit under state law and/or other local codes" or "[t]wo persons in a studio unit, three persons in a one-bedroom unit, four per-sons in a two-bedroom unit, six persons in a three-bedroom unit, or eight persons in a four-bedroom unit.[263]" As with the exception above, landlord is deemed in approval of such additional occupant, if failed to respond to the request, with stated reasons, within 14 days. Sec. 37.9(a)(2)(B). Note that the rule on adding relatives, Rule 6.15D, does not have an option for an occupant to be deemed approved "by the open and established behavior of the parties," something available under Rules 6.15A, B, and E.

(v) When the tenants add occupants in amounts over the limits stated in the lease agreement. Sec. 37.9(a)(2)(C). This is part of the modifications, which became effective since November 9, 2015. Rules on handling such additional occupants, Nos. 6.15A, 6.15B, 6.15D, were amended, and the Rule 6.15E was added to cover procedural steps for both sides of the transaction. The standards of landlord's approval are similar, although there are differences: e.g., the above-noted carve-out for 6.15D not including "open and established behavior," or the requirement under 6.15B to make a request prior to commencement of the proposed occupancy.

(c) Statement of the grounds—what is the breach of a covenant.

Like every notice under the Rent Ordinance, this notice requires a statement of its grounds for eviction.[264] For the notice drafter to decide on how to define the subject breach, it helps to see it from the court's perspective, how the allegation of breach stated in the notice can later be proved at trial.

The standard for finding of the breach was stated in *Asell v. Rodrigues* (1973) 32 Cal.App.3d 817, 823-824: "In determining whether a landlord has probable cause to believe that a tenant has breached the lease, the court must apply an objective standard, *i.e.*, would a reasonable and prudent lessor, under similar circumstances and knowing what the lessor in question knows, have concluded that the tenant had violated the covenants of the lease."

The breach generally had to be a material violation, and with the November 2015 update of the Ordinance, it is now expressly required that "the violation was substantial.[265]" Landlords may offer a counter-argument that an intentional breach of any degree is usually actionable.[266]

Of course, in the context of an eviction notice, the element of lessor's knowledge of the breach is directly connected to the issue of waiver— whether the landlord accepted rent, while knowing about the breach. See the waiver defense discussion under the previously discussed rent causes, ¶ II(1)(g) and ¶ II(3)(d).

(d) Timing—no one-year limit.

While the action for non-payment of rent must be brought within one year, no such time limitation applies to an eviction under CCP §1161(3).[267]

(e) Application of Rule 12.20.

Rule 12.20 had been significantly reworked in 2011, aimed at limiting subsequent changes of the terms of the lease.[268] The implication of the new Rule 12.20 on this type of eviction was that the landlord could not evict for a violation of a term changed or non-existent at the time the lease commenced.[269] Terms added or changed in compliance with the Rule 12.20, are still actionable under this 37.9(a)(2) ground. In 2017, the interpretation of what changes are in compliance with 12.20 was significantly enlarged, albeit by an unpublished decision in *Kardosh*.[133]

(f) Other required elements.

Other terms, clauses, and issues are similar to the 3-day notice for non-payment of rent [¶ II(1)(e), *supra*], except that a copy of the notice together with its proof of service has to be filed with the Rent Board. Notice of an option to request initial inspection does not apply.

(g) Worth noting.

Besides Rules 6.15A–E regulating the issue of subletting on the citywide level, there are statewide statutes worth noting, such as: Cal. Civ. Code §§ 1995.210–230, allowing to put restrictions on transferring interest in the lease, even an absolute prohibition, instructing to construe an ambiguity in the lease regarding such restriction in favor of transferability, and stating that absence of a such prohibition in the lease means a right of unrestricted transfer. See also, Cal. Civ. Code § 1954.53(d).

(h) Section 8 application.

A material or repeated violation of the lease terms is a valid ground for terminating a Section 8 lease. In fact, it is the first ground mentioned in the statute.[270] The time length for the eviction notice, however, may be increased to 30 days, depending on the federal program in use and the language of the lease.[154]

A. Volkov. Eviction Notice In San Francisco.

5. Nuisance, causing substantial damage, or creating a substantial interference with the comfort, safety or enjoyment of the property. SFRO § 37.9(a)(3).

(a) Type and Length of the Notice: either a 3-day notice to cure or quit, under CCP § 1161(3), or a 3-day notice to quit (no opportunity to cure), under CCP § 1161(4), depending on circumstances.

CCP § 1161(4) does not mention a requirement for the notice to be in writing, but Section 37.9(c) does, and, since the notice has to be served in compliance with CCP § 1162, and later proved as so made and served, landlords may not opt to giving an oral termination notice.

Another difference between (3) and (4) subsections of CCP § 1161 is now that, effective September 1, 2019, the notice under (3) need to exclude from its 3-day count "Saturdays and Sundays and other judicial holidays," while the notice under (4) does not.

(b) Statement of nature of nuisance, damage, or interference is required.

The requirement to state the nature of offense under this ground is expressed in the ground itself [Section 37.9(a)(3)], in Section 37.9(c), and in the "Fact Sheet 4" Rent Board publication. None of these three explain what it means.

Available case law suggests that there has to be a statement of "necessary facts.[271]" A Federal, yet San Francisco, case explores further into what facts are sufficient as necessary and what would be an adequate notice under 37.9(a)(3): to identify the specific conduct, the location of the events, the alleged victim or the time or the date of the alleged conduct.[272] Note that the decision lists last three elements disjunctively. A follow-up decision puts the elements conjunctively in another San Francisco *Swords to Plowshares* case,[273] where it holds: "if a tenancy is terminated based upon specific incidents violating the lease agreement, Section 247.4(a) requires that the notice of termination include details about the incidents including times, places, and alleged victims."

At least in one trial-court level S.F. case, a date period stated in the notice as "from on or before [certain date] to present ..." was found sufficient.[274]

Since the amendment of this eviction ground on November 9, 2015, it is now required that the complained-about "activities are severe, continuing, or recurring in nature." The Ordinance now expressly reads

the kinds of actionable violations disjunctively, so the previously emp-
loyed tenants' argument that the violation has to be ongoing is no
longer valid—the violation can be severe and take place only once.
A landlord may also cite a known rule for adjudicating short-term, but
reoccurring conduct as "capable of repetition, yet evading review,[275]"
especially if the complained-about conduct is a matter of public
concern.[276]

(c) What is nuisance and when the property damage is waste.

"Anything which is injurious to health, ... or is indecent or offensive
to the senses, or an obstruction to the free use of property, so as to
interfere with the comfortable enjoyment of life or property ... is a
nuisance." Cal. Civ. Code § 3479.

While nuisance is at least generally defined by a statute, the waste is
not.[277] "Waste occurs when the market value of property is substantially
or permanently diminished or depreciated.[278]" In relation to finding of
waste, "permanent" does not mean absolutely incurable, it only means
that, if not cured, the injury to the property would permanently remain
present.[279] Note that for satisfying this cause for eviction under the Rent
Ordinance, a landlord only needs the "substantial damage," not necessarily permanent.

Evicting parties, as always, should expect proving their allegations later
in court, including the circumstances and particulars of the offense as
stated in the notice. Some nuisances are hard to prove. For instance, it
is better to have several witnesses to testify in support of a smell
nuisance.[280]

It is a bit easier to prove a noise nuisance. For instance, how a landlord
would prove barking? By introducing a sound recording into evidence.[281]
In *Wilms*, it was held that the court was correct in admitting into evidence a sound recording of a barking dog. While a sound recording was
found applicable to prove noise, both landlords and tenants have to be
aware that recording anyone without disclosure may lead to a criminal
liability.[282] This brings us to a conclusion that sound recording is admis-
sible to show noise levels (as it was of a barking dog in *Wilms*), but
would be inadmissible when constitutes anything more than just noise,
such as a conversation where spoken words can be recognized.

If a particular nuisance case involves unsanitary condition of the
property, it might come handy to know that the San Francisco Penal

Code imposes a duty on the lower unit's tenants to upkeep the nearest sidewalk.[283]

(d) When the notice is issued without alternative to cure.

There are circumstances when the notice under this Section requires no alternative to cure to be given to a tenant. It relates to incurable breaches of a covenant in the lease,[284] including nuisance and waste.

CCP § 1161(4) instructs that when a tenant conducts nuisance or commits waste (s)he "*thereby* terminates the lease, and the landlord ... shall ... be entitled to restitution of possession..." The lease is thus terminated by the act itself and this is why under those circumstances no opportunity to cure is required in the notice—the lease is already terminated and there is nothing to cure.

(e) Limitations under 37.9(a)(3.1)(A)—(F).

The Rent Ordinance expressly limits application of this cause for eviction against victims of acts of domestic violence, as explained under Section § 37.9(a)(3.1). See also, CC § 1946.7.

It is important to observe that sub-section 3.2 imposes, with certain exceptions, a duty of strict confidentiality of information relevant to the issues defined under sub-section 3.1, received in confidence by a landlord from a tenant, or tenant's household member.

(f) Timing—no one-year limit.

While the action for non-payment of rent must be brought within one year, no such time limitation applies to an eviction under CCP § 1161(3).[267] There is no such limitation in CCP § 1161(4) either.

And while there is no formal time limit, there are at least two informal ones. One comes from the discussed earlier issue of waiver or estoppel, where a landlord knowingly accepts rent after the tenant's committed act of nuisance, property damage, or other act of waste. Another limitation comes from the landlords' duty of care to their tenants. Unlike most other just causes for eviction, where the decision to commence an action and issue the notice is entirely within the landlord's choice, it can be argued here that it is the landlord's duty to promptly address instances of nuisance.[285] It is clearly beneficial for a landlord not to delay issuance of notice under this section.

(g) Other required elements.

Other terms, clauses, and issues are similar to the 3-day notice for non-payment of rent, [¶ II(1)(e), *supra*], except that a copy of the notice for this eviction together with its proof of service has to be filed with the Rent Board. Notice of an option to request initial inspection does not apply.

(h) Section 8 application.

Commission of nuisance, property damage, or waste is a valid ground for terminating a Section 8 lease. If the violation constitutes a tenant's violation of "federal, State, or local law that imposes obligations on the tenant in connection with the occupancy or use of the premises," it comes under 24 CFR 982.310(a)(2). Tenants or their families' "history of disturbance of neighbors or destruction of property, or of living or housekeeping habits resulting in damage to the unit or premises,[286]" is an expressly acknowledged "other good cause" for eviction under 24 CFR 982.310(a)(3). Particulars of the violation are similarly required to be present in the notice.[287]

The time length for the eviction notice may be increased from the state-required 3 days to the federally required 30 days, depending on the federal program in use and language of the lease.[154]

6. Using a rental unit for an illegal purpose. SFRO § 37.9(a)(4).

(a) Type and Length of the Notice: either a 3-day notice to quit (no opportunity to cure), under CCP § 1161(4), or a 30-day notice to cure or quit, if the eviction ground is for the first-time violation of Chapter 41A.

A recent amendment to Section 37.9(a)(4) required a 30-day notice, instead of a 3-day one, for letting a tenant to cure tenant's first violation of Chapter 41A. Chapter 41A applies to all residencies since February 2015.[288]

(b) When applicable.

This is a catch-all ground for all for-fault evictions not specifically addressed in other enumerated causes. And it is safe to guess, due to expressly mentioned short-term rentals [under the first 2015 amendment, adding 37.9(a)(4)**(A)**], that an eviction for this activity falls squarely within the same just cause. An exception added by a later 2015 amendment [37.9(a)(4)(B)] now prohibits an eviction for using a property as a "residential occupancy of a unit not authorized for residential occupancy by the City."

An "illegal purpose" can be found in tenant's using property in violation of local laws and regulations, including ones regulating operation of "a bed-and-breakfast facility and/or a transient occupancy residential structure," or short-term rentals.[289]

Technically, the term "illegal" means not only a violation of law or an administrative regulation, but also a breach of a lease contract. This includes tenancies pursuant to a settlement agreement between a tenant and a landlord, which is also a contract.[290] The contract is the law, binding its parties to perform their obligations,[291] therefore a breach of any contractual term is an illegal activity *per se*. The "illegal purpose" can also be found even if a landlord previously agreed to such illegal use or tenant's conduct, because the agreed-upon term is illegal and, thus, void and unenforceable.[292]

But since "[a] lease constitutes both a conveyance of a leasehold interest and a contract,[293]" a violation of a lease covenant can be covered under Section 37.9(a)(2), and the tenant's conduct causing nuisance, waste, or property damage is addressed by Section 37.9(a)(3). The choice will also reflect on curability of the notice, more likely being a "cure of quit" under Sections 37.9(a)(2) and 37.9(a)(3), and simply a "quit" one under Section 37.9(a)(4).

A description of the subject violation will be required to satisfy the requirements of "an adequate notice" discussed above under 37.9(a)(3): to identify the specific conduct, the location of the events, the alleged victim or the time or date of the alleged conduct.[272]

(c) Illegal conduct must relate to the use of premises.

The conduct must be one related to the unlawful use of leased premises. Tenants argue that some entirely unrelated, yet illegal activity may not be a subject for eviction, *i.e.*, tenant's drunk driving or receiving a parking ticket. However, there is no requirement for a landlord to demonstrate an injury in fact. If subject conduct is connected with the use of property, this should be a reason sufficient enough for the landlord to undertake the eviction under this cause.

(d) When the notice is issued without an alternative to cure.

The notice under this Section requires no alternative to cure given to the tenant, except when the eviction is for the first violation of S.F. Admin. Code, Chapter 41A.

CCP § 1161(4) instructs that when a tenant is "using the premises for an unlawful purpose," (s)he "*thereby* terminates the lease, and the landlord ... shall ... be entitled to restitution of possession..." The lease in such situations is terminated by the act itself; this is why, under those circumstances, no opportunity to cure is required in the notice—the lease is already terminated, and there is nothing to cure.

As mentioned above, one kind of conduct is required to be stated in the alternative, it is the first instance of a tenant violating S.F. Admin. Code, Chapter 41A. This notice is also required to provide 30 days for a tenant to cure the violation.

(e) Timing—no one-year limit.

While the action for non-payment of rent must be brought within one year, no such time limitation applies to an eviction under CCP § 1161(3) or CCP § 1161(4).

Like with the nuisance or waste evictions, there are reasons for a landlord not to delay an eviction for too long after discovering premises' use for unlawful purposes, because of the discussed earlier issues of waiver and estoppel, where a landlord knowingly accepts rent after the tenant's committed act of nuisance, property damage, or other act of waste. It is also because landlords may be held liable to other tenants, or neighbors. There can even be a case of a civil or criminal landlords' liability for the conduct of their tenants, for example, when a tenant uses the premises for an illegal commercial cultivating of marijuana on the premises.

(f) Other required elements.

Other terms, clauses, and issues are similar to the 3-day notice for non-payment of rent, [¶ II(1)(e), *supra*], except that a copy of the notice for this eviction together with its proof of service has to be filed with the Rent Board. Notice of an option to request initial inspection does not apply.

(g) Section 8 application.

Unlawful use of leased premises is a valid ground for terminating a Section 8 lease. If the violation constitutes tenant's violation "federal, State, or local law that imposes obligations on the tenant in connection with the occupancy or use of the premises," it is covered under 24 CFR 982.310(a)(2).

Evictions for criminal activity are covered under 24 CFR 982.310(c). This sub-section also covers activities *near* the premises, and includes activities by tenant's guests and other persons in tenant's control.[294] Time period for the notice may be 30 days.[154]

7. Failure to renew a terminated lease. SFRO § 37.9(a)(5).

I categorize this eviction as a "for-fault" type, since it suggests tenant's failure or refusal to renew a terminated lease. However, the court in *Binkerfield v City of Berkeley*, placed this eviction in a third category, along with for-fault and non-fault evictions.[295] This categorization does not affect our analysis of the notice requirements.

(a) Type and Length of the Notices. There are two stages of notices involved here: the first stage is when a written demand to review or extend the lease agreement is made, this one is served 30 or 60 days prior to the expiration of the lease, with additional time allotted for the service of the demand; the second stage is the actual eviction notice in case of the tenant's refusal to renew.

For certain exempt rental units, there is no eviction notice required, and the landlord may directly proceed with the unlawful detainer under CCP § 1161(1). If the unit is not exempt, tenants from such non-exempt units may not be evicted without a notice their tenancy being terminated.[296] Remember that a tenant by sufferance is also included in the definition of the "Tenant" under the Rent Ordinance.[297]

Among the non-exempt units, those where the lease has an express provision for renewal, either a 3-day notice to cure or quit under CCP § 1161(3), or a 3-day notice to quit under CCP § 1161(4) is applicable. A renewal clause is deemed to be a substantial element of the lease,[298] and is read-in to the leases by courts when there is ambiguity or uncertainty on this subject, interpreting the clause in favor of the tenant.[299]

For non-exempt units with no express provision for default for non-renewal of the lease, assuming that lease is not susceptible to an attack on ambiguity or uncertainty on this term, a 60-day notice to vacate is applicable, declaring that termination took place on the expiration date of the original lease agreement (not on expiration day of the notice). Landlords should abstain from collecting rent during the time the notice is pending[300] (rent payments tendered during the notice time shall be returned to the tenant within 30 days from the tender[254]).

Landlords who plan on using or including such express provisions for renewal in their leases, should consider conditions imposed by CC §1945.5, requiring that this clause has to be made "in at least eight-point boldface type" in the body of the contract and then repeated in no less than the same size boldface type "immediately prior to the place where the lessee

executes the agreement." If those drafting precautions are being complied with, the rest is defined by a simple fact, whether the landlord accepted a rent payment for any term following the expiration of the lease. If
yes, the contract is presumed renewed, typically as a month-to-month
lease.[301] If not, and the tenant was offered and refused to renew the
lease, an eviction is allowed under this Section.

Parties should pay additional attention to the language of the original lease, to see if it contained any provisions describing what happens after the
expiration of the initial term, such as converting it to a month-to-month
lease. If there is a provision of that kind, tenants may argue that their
"right to a re-lease of the property in accordance with the agreement of
the parties should not be cut off because of any alleged failure on [their]
part either to give oral notice or in every instance to technically specify
the exact nature of the instrument by which the tenant should remain in
the possession and enjoyment of the premises.[302]" The landlords may
argue that holding over is not sufficient to extend the lease.[303]

(b) Written notice is still required.

It might appear that Section 37.9(a)(5) is a cause for eviction where no
eviction notice may be required,[304] albeit under a narrowly defined set
of circumstances. Yet some written notification is most likely involved.

First, it may apply only for the types of property falling under S.F. Admin
Code, Section 37.2(r) definitions of the types of real property exempt
from the definition of a "rental unit," mainly Sections 37.2(r)(5), (6), and
(7): single-family houses or condominium units and buildings with either
a certificate of occupancy issued after the effective date of the ordinance, or those undergone substantial rehabilitation after that date.[305]

The second requirement is embedded in a scenario under Sec. 37.9(a)(5),
it is that the parties are still under a fixed-term lease. Generally, a tenancy for a fixed period of time requires no termination notice and terminates on its own, giving a landlord the right to re-enter the property.[306]

The third fact to establish is whether the landlord did not treat the tenancy as one requiring a termination notice (*i.e.*, as a month-to-month
tenancy, rather than a fixed-term one). This will include landlord's
conduct under any of the statutes requiring notice for termination.[307]

However, S.F. Admin. Code, Section 37.9(c) requires that "the landlord
informs the tenant *in writing* on or before the date upon which notice

to vacate is given of the grounds under which possession is sought, ... before endeavoring to recover possession." This means that, unless the subject tenancy is exempt from Section 37.9, a written notice shall be issued in connection with the invoked eviction ground, in this case the refusal to renew a lease.

(c) Required elements to satisfy the cause for eviction under 37.9(a)(5).

The language of this section establishes the following requisite elements:

- there has to be "a written request or demand by the landlord to execute a written extension or renewal thereof for a further term of like duration ..." Notice that the initial lease agreement can be either oral or written, but the demand to renew must be in writing;

- the proposed extension or renewal must be made "under such terms which are materially the same as in the previous agreement." See also a discussion on the modern version of the Rule 12.20,[268] narrowing the ways how the terms of the preexisting lease can be changed; and

- the proposed terms must "not conflict with any of the provisions of this Chapter." This is a Rent Board's hint to the landlords anticipating to offer a renewal to check the language of their lease against the current version of Chapter 37.9, to adjust non-conforming provisions. This is also an argument against practice of offering renewals, because the original lease would be more likely interpreted in compliance with the Chapter's version then in effect, while the newly renewed lease would have to match the current version, and the Chapter is rarely amended to benefit a landlord.

(d) Timing—not to soon and not too late.

In theory, all a landlord has to do is to ensure not to miss the date when the old fixed-term lease expires, to have the tenant to sign a new fixed-term lease. This way, at the end of that fixed term, a land-lord can evict, provided that the unit and other prerequisites fit the bill. For the month-to-month and lesser term tenancies, the shortest notice of change is "not less than seven days before the expiration of a term.[308]" If new terms involve an increase in rent payment less than 10%, the time is 30 days, plus additional time for service under CCP § 1013[309]; if for more than 10% increase in rent—additional 30 days.[310] The annual rent increase for rent-controlled units had never yet reached a 10% mark,[311] however, a property exempt from the rent-control, such as a single-family house or a condominium, can be adjusted to the new market level rent, and the market level does go over a 10% rate of annual increase quite often.

It will be thus prudent to serve a written demand for renewal of the lease at least 60 days prior to its expiration, with additional time added depending on the matter of service.

An eviction notice—or the unlawful detainer action in those cases where no notice was required—following tenant's refusal to renew, should not be served too long after the expiration of the original lease, because the refusing tenant will most likely tender the next month's rent payment, which the landlord would not accept. Yet the landlord should neither "[r]efuse to accept or acknowledge receipt of a tenant's lawful rent payment," nor "[r]efuse to cash a rent check for over 30 days.[254]" It thus follows that the eviction under Section 37.9(a)(5) shall commence within the first 30 days following the expiration of the original lease (if no rent payment is offered), or within the 30 days following tenant's tender of a rent payment past that expiration. Landlords shall be prepared to argue that no new tenancy is created by holding over without consent.[303]

(e) Other required elements.

If there is a notice involved, its required elements will be the same as those required under the applicable statute, such as CCP §§ 1161(3) or (4), for the 3-day notices [see, ¶ II(1)(e), *supra*], or to contain elements similar to those discussed above for the notices issued under CC § 1946, § 1946.1, for the 30/60-day notice to vacate [¶ II(2)(g), *supra*]. A copy of the notice together with its proof of service has to be filed with the Rent Board, and the filing would include the preceding written landlord's demand to renew the lease. Notice of an option to request initial inspection should be included in the 60-day notice to vacate [¶ I(K)].

(f) Section 8 application.

Tenant's refusal to renew the lease is a valid ground for terminating a Section 8 lease. It is covered under 24 CFR 982.310(a)(3) as "[o]ther good cause," with the definition including "[f]ailure by the family to accept the offer of a new lease or revision.[312]"

(g) Landlord's refusal to renew.

Since the initial written demand to renew may start a negotiation process between the parties, it is important to consider the other potential scenario—landlord's own refusal to renew the lease.

Effective January 1, 2014, a landlord may not terminate a lease or fail to renew it, if the tenants are protected under provisions of CCP § 1161.3 for issues related to domestic violence, sexual assault, stalking, human trafficking, elderly abuse, or abuse of a dependent adult, unless the prescribed procedures are followed and the defenses referenced in the statute do not bar the eviction.

In the context of a government-subsidized property, such as Section 8, if the landlord terminates or fails to renew a contract (here, with the applicable sponsoring government authority), a 90-day notice has to be given.[313]

8. Refusing access to a rental unit. SFRO § 37.9(a)(6).

Historically, landlord's right to reenter leased premises was the first concept developed in the landlord-tenant law, with the earliest known statute addressing the issue enacted in the 1328 Statute of Northhampton.[8]

(a) Type and Length of the Notices. This cause of eviction may involve the most amount of sequential notices; there could be from one to as many as three: the initial notice of intent to enter, the notice to cease refusing access, if entry was denied, and, finally, an eviction notice, if a tenant still continues to refuse access. For most instances, a 3-Day Cure or Quit Notice under CCP § 1161(3) is appropriate.

First notice is given pursuant to CC § 1954, unless: there is an emergency, the tenant is present and consents to entry, or the tenant abandons the rented unit.[314] When this (first) notice is due, it is almost always required to be in writing, except when the tenant consents to an oral notice, or when the entry is for the purpose of showing the unit to prospective purchasers, and a written notice was previously served within 120 days preceding the subject oral notice.[315] CC § 1954(d)(1) provides for the required contents in the notice, and what is considered a reasonable time for service of notice prior to entry. The statute suggests that 24 hours before entry "shall be presumed to be reasonable notice in absence of evidence to the contrary." (*Id.*) San Francisco Rent Board "Topic No. 252[316]" deals away with both the presumption and the contrary evidence, it just states that "[t]enants must be provided with at least 24-hours written notice before the landlord enters the unit," which seems to narrow the landlord's right to entry from what is provided in the statute. However, the "Topic" is more of a commentary, it is not a part of the ordinance or the Rules.

Second notice is issued in case the tenant refuses access to the unit. It will be the first notice when the initial notice of intent to enter under CC § 1954 was oral or not required under the three exceptions mentioned above. This notice is required to be given in writing by the express wording of the Rent Ordinance: "[t]he tenant has, *after written notice to cease*, refused the landlord access to the rental unit ..." SFRO § 37.9(a)(6).

How to deal with tenant's refusal of access depends on what are the terms of the lease agreement. If the provisions for granting or refusing access were set in the lease, no further analysis is required. If the lease is silent on the issue, argument has to be made that the landlord's right to entry is provided by statute, and thus implied in the lease.[317] Notice is to be drafted as a 3-Day Notice to Cure or Quit, under CCP § 1161(3), where the cure is to cease refusing access to the property. Effective September 1, 2019, calculation of time for a 3-day notice under CCP § 1161(3) "exclud[es] Saturdays and Sundays and other judicial holidays."

(b) Required elements to satisfy the cause for eviction under 37.9(a)(6).

Include a fully restated request for entry under CC § 1954 in the eviction notice. Since the eviction notice is still a request for entry, it has to comply with both CCP § 1161(3) and CC § 1954.

Besides requirements addressed above, two additional requisite elements are that the access is sought (i) "as required by state or local law" [Section 37.9(a)(6)], meaning that the requested access is reasonable, within the purposes defined in CC § 1954, not in abuse of the right to access or for harassment of the tenant,[318] and (ii) not in "a significant and intentional violation of Section 1954.[319]"

A recent case analyzing reasonability of an access request and tenant's denial of entry, held that requesting access during a weekend still can be treated as one made during "normal business hours" as required by CC § 1954.[320]

(c) Timing—denial of entry better be addressed immediately.

There is no room for delaying action under this cause for eviction, for several reasons. The need to entry may either disappear (and so is gone the landlord's right to request entry for that need), or the need may be urgent (for instance, the landlord's duty to make repairs and accommodate these of other occupants of the building, neighbors, or government authorities demanding immediate cure of some violation or condition). Further, if the issue is not addressed within the month when the refuse of entry had taken place, and the rent is accepted for the following month, a tenant may argue waiver or promissory estoppel next time this issue comes around.

(d) Other required elements.

Other required elements will be the same as those required under the applicable statute, such as CCP §§ 1161(3), for the 3-day notices [see, ¶ II(1)(e), supra]. A copy of the notice together with its proof of service has to be filed with the Rent Board, and the filing would include all the preceding notices, including (if done separately) a written to cease refusing access.

(e) Section 8 application.

If the refusal of access is defined under the terms of the lease, eviction is allowed under 24 CFR 982.310 (a)(1), as a "repeated violation of the terms and conditions of the lease." It thus must be repeated before it becomes ripe for an eviction cause, just as it is the case with eviction under Section 37.9(a)(6). If the term is not sufficiently defined, then 24 CFR 982.310 (a)(2) seems applicable (a violation of law). See discussion of reasonability under *Dromy v. Lukovsky*.[320]

9. Possession of a unit by a tenant not approved by a landlord. SFRO § 37.9(a)(7).

(a) Type and Length of the Notice. One of three different notices may apply:

(i) 3-Day Notice to Quit. If the remaining occupant was placed on premises by the vacated approved tenants, then a 3-Day Notice To Quit addressed to those approved tenants, but including all occupants claiming any possession right under their tenancy, issued under CCP § 1161(4) ["Any tenant, subtenant, ... assigning or subletting ... contrary to the conditions or covenants of his or her lease ... or using the premises for an unlawful purpose, thereby terminates the lease."]. Note that this subletting violation is actionable here (under Section 37.9(a)(7)), while it is generally *not* actionable under Section 37.9(a)(2)(A) and (B), where at least some original or approved tenant still remains on the premises, except when the landlord has not "unreasonably withheld the right to sublet following a written request by the tenant."

(ii) 5-Day Notice to Quit under Forcible Detainer. If a person unlawfully enters into possession during absence of a lawful possessor, one who "within five days preceding such unlawful entry, was in the peaceable and undisturbed possession" of the property, then the lawful possessor, may demand his possession back by a 5-Day notice.[321] Note that this kind of notice has a defined time limit, within which the intruder was entering the property to claim possession. "Flat breach of peace is not required,[322]" yet "a mere trespass" is not enough.[323] A holding over and refusal to leave were held sufficiently plead to support a 5-day demand,[324] as well as occupant's refusal to leave after a license was revoked.[325]

(iii) No-delay, "immediate" notice. If the remaining occupant has no relation to the vacated approved tenants, and was not assigned or sublet to by them, then a written notice is applicable to inform vacated approved tenants about the grounds, upon which the landlord is commencing an eviction of the holding-over unapproved tenant.[328] There is no opportunity to cure given in this notice, and no requirement to provide for any particular length of time to vacate. Analyze if remaining occupants are tenants at sufferance, this scenario may be inapplicable.[297]

(iv) No 30- or 60-day notices under CC § 1946 or § 1946.1. This is because those two statutes are for terminating established tenancies, "a hiring of residential real property." Vice versa, if the target occupant had **hired** the real property from the evictor, that occupant is then an approved tenant, and this cause for eviction is inapplicable.

(v) An optional route for a landlord is to proceed by way of eject-ment action: "pros" of this route is to avoid strict unlawful detainer statute and requirements of notice; "cons" is to prosecute the action in general civil forum, based on 30-day summons and with no advantages of a summary action.[326]

(b) Applicable grounds.

This allowed cause for eviction addresses an issue of holdover or trespass by occupants not approved by the landlord. CCP § 1161(1) contemplates the situation when "he or she continues in possession ... by subtenant ... after the expiration of the term for which it is let to him or her; provided the expiration is of a nondefault nature however brought about without the permission of his or her landlord ..."

Generally, no notice would be required under CCP § 1161(1),[327] in absence of the Rent Ordinance. However, the Rent Ordinance requires to inform the "tenant" in writing about the grounds in *each* utilized eviction cause.[328] A "tenant" is "[a] person entitled by written or oral agreement, sub-tenancy approved by the landlord, or by sufferance, to occupy a residential dwelling unit to the exclusion of others.[329]"
A "tenant at sufferance" is a tenant, who previously occupied under a lease agreement, now holding over the expiration of his/her original lease.[330]

Therefore, to determine if the eviction on this ground can proceed, and under what kind of a notice, a 2-step analysis applies:

First step is to decide, which one, out of the three scenarios, is present. Hint: only the third one will allow an eviction to proceed under this cause:

1) if the person remaining in possession falls under the definition of a "tenant" under Section 37.2(t), or an approved occupant,[331] then this eviction cause may not apply;

2) if the person in possession is not a "tenant," but a "tenant" is still residing on the property, then this eviction cause is unavailable, too.

However, if that residing "tenant" is not an original tenant, and the additional occupant is "not approved" under Rules 6.14 and 6.15A, B, D, or E, then an eviction under 37.9(a)(2) may apply (see, ¶ II(4), above);

3) if the person in possession is not a "tenant," and all "tenants" had vacated, then an eviction may commence against that remaining possessor, with a preliminary written notice to a "tenant."

Proceed to read below, to see if your lease and the facts about the eviction in question may construe a tenant as "not approved" under Rules 6.14 and 6.15A, B, D, or E.

If all the remaining residents of the subject property are "not approved" tenants, the second step is to determine whether their occupancy can be deemed in violation of a condition or covenant of the lease. The answer to this question defines the length and type of the notice.

Assuming that the third scenario from the first step above confirms with the requirements of CCP § 1161(4), a 3-Day Notice to Quit can be issued to the vacated tenants—not to the unapproved occupants. Read below on the subject of approval.

(c) Defining a "not approved" tenant and an occupancy running "contrary to the conditions or covenants of his or her lease."

(I) Under Rules 6.14 and 6.15A, B, D, and E.

Rent Ordinance Rules and Regulations, Rules 6.14 and 6.15, define whether the remaining occupant is not approved by the landlord and how to treat a "no subletting" clause in the lease. The Rent Board is within its rights to amend its Ordinance by the Rules.[332] While these Rules may seem to conflict in part with the statewide Civil Code § 1954.53 for regulating and limiting the landlord's right to increase rent, there is no conflict for the eviction purposes.[333]

Rule 6.14 groups all occupancies by time: before January 1, 1996, after January 1, 1996, but where the last original occupant vacated before April 25, 2000, and after January 1, 1996, and where the last original occupant vacated on or after April 25, 2000.[334] The rule deals with subsequent occupants and "co-occupants," but only unapproved subsequent occupants may be evicted under the subject 37.9(a)(7) ground. Co-occupants are defined in Rule 6.14 as ones having an agreement directly with the owner (Rule 6.14(a)(3)).

A. Volkov. Eviction Notice In San Francisco.

The procedure to establish the landlord's right *to raise rent* differs between these three groups, but there is no difference for the purposes of evicting under Section 37.9(a)(7). The only way a landlord may still evict under Section 37.9(a)(7) is if the landlord had no "actual know-ledge" of that occupancy "within a reasonable time." Absence of actual knowledge can be of two kinds: when a landlord does not know about another resident at all, or when a landlord denied a request to add a resident, and did not know that the resident was added despite landlord's withholding consent. This withholding of consent needs to satisfy conditions under Rules 6.15A, B, D, or E for not being deemed unreasonable.

Any other scenario bars the eviction under section 37.9(a)(7), because:

either the landlord knew about the occupancy, but failed to inform the subsequent occupant about the landlord's election not to treat that occupant as approved (the occupant is then deemed approved), and the landlord waived his rights or consented to the occupancy— eviction under the subject cause is not allowed; or

the landlord knew and did serve the so-called "6.14" notice, which requires to inform that "when the last of the original occupant(s) vacates the premises, a new tenancy is created for purposes of determining the rent under the Rent Ordinance." The served notice therefore would create a presumption of the occupant being app-roved (albeit with a chance to raise rent), and an eviction under Section 37.9(a)(7) would not be applicable.

Under Rules 6.15A, B, D and E, landlord's withholding of consent may be deemed unreasonable, thus deeming an otherwise unauthorized occupant as authorized.

Rule 6.15A establishes requirements when and how a landlord may have an "absolute prohibition against subletting or assignment." If the absolute prohibition clause is present in the lease and is still enforceable, breach of that covenant will support an eviction of an original tenant-breachor, under Section 37.9(a)(2) [¶ II(4)]. If someone else is still left in possession, the same clause and its violation will support an eviction under the subject Section 37.9(a)(7) of other occupants, who are not otherwise approved by the landlord and who would be in possession of the rental unit after all original/approved tenants moved out.

A landlord may lose a right to evict under 6.15A, if the occupant in question would be deemed approved by the landlord. The court in *Danekas v. S. F. Rent Board* held that interpretation of the rule may determine the tenant's status: "[t]he "right to sublet" referred to in the second condition is not one conferred by the landlord, as appellant contends. It is decreed in the ordinance, even in the face of a lease clause to the contrary.[335]"

This happens when:

(1) [for any assignment or subletting] "the landlord fails to respond in writing within fourteen (14) days of actual receipt of written notice" of the tenant's "initial written request to the landlord for permission to sublease" made "in accordance with Section 37.9(a)(2)(A)." Rule 6.15A(c); or

(2) [for a partial assignment or subletting] landlord's refusal was unreasonable. Rule 6.15A(d). Rule 6.15A(d)(1) provides seven factors of what can make the refusal unreasonable, and the factors appear to be conjunctive rather than disjunctive, requiring satisfaction of all seven of them.[336] Rule 6.15A(d)(1)(i)–(vii). Subsection 6.15A(e)(1)–(5) lists five non-inclusive factors, under which landlord's refusal is not considered unreasonable.

Rule 6.15B applies when the no-subletting clause in the lease is not "absolute," but requires landlord's consent. Although the language of Rule 6.15B is drafted to protect a tenant against an eviction under Section 37.9(a)(2), it applies to Section 37.9(a)(7) in the part where it defines under what circumstances an occupant is deemed approved. For purposes of the discussed eviction cause, these circumstances are spelled out as seven factors, Rule 6.15B(c)(1)(i)–(vii), under which landlord's withholding of consent to subletting or assignment is deemed unreasonable. Scenarios, where landlord's refusal is not deemed unreasonable, include, "but not limited to" the five factors listed under Rule 6.15B(d)(1)–(5).

Rule 6.15C is not applicable to this eviction cause. For the commentary, read *Foster v. Britton* (2015) 242 Cal. App. 4th 920.

Rule 6.15D regulates tenant's requests to move-in a relative, such as "the tenant's child, parent, grandchild, grandparent, brother or sister, or the spouse or the domestic partner (as defined in Administrative

Code Sections 62.1 through 62.8) of such relatives, or the spouse or domestic partner of the tenant." Rule 6.15D(a).

In a fashion similar to Rules 6.15A and B, it provides factors, under which landlord's withholding of consent is deemed unreasonable; there are six factors here. Rule 6.15D(c)(1)–(6). And the five factors exemplifying landlord's refusal as not unreasonable are listed in 6.15D(d)(1)–(5).

However, there is an important distinction of Rule 6.15D from A, B, and E, it is that "the open and established behavior" is not sufficient for a subtenant-relative to be deemed approved by the landlord.

Rule 6.15E is recently added, effective December 4, 2015. It addresses a situation when "a tenant who resides in the unit requests the landlord's permission to add an additional occupant to the rental unit that will exceed the number of people allowed by the lease or rental agreement." Landlord's refusal to approve such additional occupant is deemed unreasonable under the factors listed in Rule 6.15E(c)(1)–(6). And there are eight examples of grounds, under which landlord's disapproval is not unreasonable: Rule 6.15E(d)(1)–(8).

Under all four Rules 6.15 A, B, D, and E, a tenant may make a written request for a new occupant.[337] If the landlord fails to respond, or responds with either an unconditional approval, or a notice explaining Rule 6.14, all these scenarios would bar an eviction under Sec. 37.9(a)(7). Only if there were no written requests made, or the landlord did not consent (in satisfaction of the factors against withholding consent unreasonably), an occupant remaining on the premises after approved occupants have vacated can still be evicted under this cause.

(II) Under terms of the original lease agreement.

Two 2015 San Francisco cases (*Mosser* and *Dropalas*) held that a minor who moved-in with his parents and continued to reside alone after the parents vacated, is an approved original occupant.[338] The court expressly limited its decision to those family members who moved-in at the commencement of the lease (*Mosser, Id.* at 516), but applications of Rules 6.14 and 6.15 may extend this holding to those subsequent co-occupants who were approved by the landlord, or deemed so approved (Both *Mosser* and *Dropalas* decisions were explained in 2017 *Danger Panda* case as limited in their finding of tenant's definition when applied to Costa Hawkins Act interpretation[339]). An unpublished case in 2017 held that determination of the occupant's status can be resolved in court without first extinguishing administrative means, although the administrative path is preferred.[340]

One more potential scenario to consider is when there is no subletting clause in the lease, or the lease is oral. The rule is that any ambiguity or uncertainty in the lease contract is construed against its drafter (typically, the landlord).[341] If a condition is absent, it won't be read into the contract by the court.[342] Therefore, without a clause prohibiting or limiting subletting or assignment, or with a clause written with ambiguity or uncertainty, the lease will be construed against the landlord, meaning in this case no prohibition on subletting or assignment. This does not entirely bar a possibility to pursue an eviction under Section 37.9(a)(7), but makes it worth considering as a material complication before commencing an eviction.

(III) If landlord accepted or demanded rent.

The general rule of thumb is that a landlord should not accept a rent payment from an unauthorized tenant, or it may otherwise create a new month-to-month tenancy under CC § 1945 (although the statute expressly applies only to a "lessee.") The landlord is not entitled to receipt of rent from a holding over occupant.[343]

CC § 1954.53(d)(4) instructs that accepting a rent "does not operate as a waiver or otherwise prevent enforcement of a covenant prohibiting sublease or assignment or as a waiver of an owner's right to establish the initial rental rate, *unless the owner has received written notice* from the tenant that is party to the agreement and thereafter accepted rent." Accord, Section 37.3(d)(2)(C). Yet, landlords are strongly advised to avoid accepting such rent payments in order to save themselves from later disputes of waiver or approval.

Under no circumstances should a landlord *request* the rent payment. If a landlord demands rent from an occupant, that occupant may no longer be evicted as a trespasser.[344]

(d) Parties to the notice.

Who is to be mentioned in the notice is a sensitive subject for this eviction. Notice should not lead to a presumption that the targeted occupant is authorized. And remember that holding over occupants require no notice, yet the original or subsequently approved ones have to be informed in writing about the eviction grounds.

The notice should include everyone known by name, along with the appropriate disclaimers, and also include unknown occupants. Follow instructions for the general element "Parties" explained in the "Commonly Required Notice Elements" chapter, ¶ I(B), above.

(e) Service of notice.

Original and subsequently authorized tenants require notice, thus they have to receive a copy. Since they are not going to be subject parties for the eviction, they require no formal service, the Rent Ordinance only demands informing them in writing. This makes it easier to achieve, *i.e.*, a copy of the notice can technically be mailed with requested mail-forwarding to the property address, and thus be forwarded and delivered to the vacated tenants.

However, it will be prudent to serve a copy by posting and mailing on the property, in full accordance with CCP § 1162. A personal service on the targeted unauthorized occupants is always desirable.

(f) An alternative—establishing new tenancy at a new rental rate. Vacancy decontrol.

Sometimes a landlord does not mind the unauthorized occupant to become an approved, paying tenant. In many instances the issue is with the vacancy decontrol: a new tenant can enter a lease on new terms, while the subsequent or continuous tenant has to be bound by the previous lease, with very little adjustments allowed under the Rent Ordinance. This mostly relates to the amount of the charged rent (Section 37.3), but other terms of the lease are also involved (Rule 12.20).

The Costa-Hawkins Act allows a landlord to establish a new rent rate for a new tenant (CC § 1954.53(a)); the same is true for a remaining occupant, when all tenants under the prior lease had vacated the property. CC § 1954.53(d)(2).[345] This creates an alternative for a landlord to establish a new level of rent with the previously unauthorized tenant.

(g) Timing.

An eviction under this cause allows for no delay. In a situation where the landlord cannot re-rent and cannot accept rent payments, the only valid reason to postpone immediate action is to make sure that all approved tenants had vacated.

"For Fault" Notices. Sec. 37.9(a)(7)

(h) Other required elements.

The notice requires several general elements discussed in the "Commonly Required Notice Elements" section of this book, including property description [¶ I(A)], contact information [¶ I(E)], statement of good faith [¶ I(F)], statement whether this notice supersedes other notices [¶ I(G)], date and signature [¶ I(H)], information about the Rent Board [¶ I(I)], notice of abandoning personal property [¶ I(J)], notice of debtor's rights [¶ I(L)], notice given in other languages, if applicable [¶ I(M)]. The statement of election of forfeiture applies when the notice is issued under CCP § 1161(4), and is to be applied with the same caution as one exercised in naming the parties, see sub-section (d) for this eviction, above. Include also the disclaimer that this notice may not be construed as approval of the target occupants.

Notice of an option to request initial inspection does not apply here. A copy of the notice together with its proof of service has to be filed with the Rent Board.

(h) Section 8 application.

Participant-tenants of a "Section 8" program may not sublease or assign their rental units, or change their primary residency away from the subject unit without notice.[346] It is the tenant's family responsibility (those family members who are under the agreement with the subsidizing governmental authority), to notify that authority "and the owner before the family moves out of the unit.[347]" The family may not be absent from the unit for more than 180 consecutive days, or it will terminate the contract.[348] Assuming that the authorized tenants under the contract had vacated, and the remaining occupants are not part of the contract, evicting those occupants will be outside of Section 8 regulations.

III. NO-FAULT EVICTIONS

First chapter of this book explored what is necessary for the so-called "for fault" eviction notices, *i.e.* notices informing about termination of a tenancy for an event triggered by a tenant's act or omission to act. This chapter covers "non-fault" eviction notices, where the termination of tenancy is happening through none of tenant's fault. For-fault and non-fault evictions are of different legislative descent: while each of the for-fault evictions has elements mandated by the municipal-level San Francisco Rent Ordinance, most of the grounds claim their roots in the statewide law. By contrast, regulations for the non-fault evictions are mostly products of local municipal legislation, with only a few provisions spelled out on a state level.[349] It thus appears that the legislative initiative in for-fault causes is a top-to-down hierarchy, while the non-fault causes result more from the grassroots' local initiatives.

Under the state law, landlord's authority to terminate a tenancy comes from Civil Code Sections 1946 and 1946.1. Readers of the earlier chapters are already familiar with these statutes from the coverage of for-fault notices taking root from the same statutes (*e.g.*, late payment of rent, (¶ II(2)). Of course, this state law is only a starting point of applicable regulations, leaving the lion's share of nuances to the local ordinances.

Common Elements And Definitions For Non-Fault Evictions.

Most of the rules previously covered are equally important to follow in crafting notices under this Chapter. Readers are advised to review Sections ¶ I (A) through (O) before proceeding with the following material.

The concepts listed here include those not previously addressed or treated differently when applied to non-fault evictions. For convenience of the reference, elements covered here are indexed in continuation of the list presented in Chapter I.

P. Absence of an opportunity to cure, or a statement in the alternative, election of forfeiture, inability to collect for pre-termination rent.

We will start with observing what elements non-fault eviction notices do not have: a declaration of forfeiture, an opportunity to cure, and a prohibition for a landlord to collect pre-termination rent.

Instead of a declaration of forfeiture due to tenant's fault, non-fault evictions cause termination (a non-renewal) of the tenancy: if an allowed ground or cause is present, then the tenancy is terminated in a certain amount of days, following service of the notice. Consequently, non-fault notices may not be stated in the alternative—there is nothing for a tenant to "cure" in order to revive the tenancy when it is terminated,[242] since there was no tenant's fault triggering it.

Also, due to the terminating nature of these evictions, non-fault notices need not to contain a declaration of forfeiture.[245] However, an unequivocal statement of terminating tenancy in still required.[213] This is often argued in practice, because the judicial form for an unlawful detainer complaint contains a field asking whether the notice "included an election of forfeiture.[350]"

Related to the issue of forfeiture is the rule that, under the non-fault kind of notice, the consequent eviction proceeding may not recover for pre-termination rent due, only to recover post-termination rental damages. This is due to the courts' interpretation of CC § 1174.[351] If this eviction requires a follow-up filing of an unlawful detainer, make sure the prayor seeks termination of the agreement, not forfeiture.[352]

The other side of this medal is that the landlord is allowed to collect rent after the notice issuance and prior to its termination.

Q. No need to follow up with another notice, except for claiming unpaid rent, or when the termination was for a temporary relocation.

General rule provides that "[a] landlord of a dwelling house who has given a month's notice under Civ. Code, § 1946, to terminate a month to month tenancy, need not, after the tenants' continuance in possession after the termination date fixed in the notice, give a further notice of three days before he may maintain an action of unlawful detainer.[353]" Do not confuse this with a situation when the tenant is also behind on rent payments, then a separate 3-day notice is required.[354]

Termination under any of the non-fault notices is a sufficient prerequisite to seek recovery of possession in court, except when the notice was issued for a *temporary* relocation, under 37.9(a)(11). Because the underlying notice was only terminating the tenancy for a definite period of time, the judgment received for enforcing such notice would also provide only for a temporary possession recovery.[355] Accordingly, practitioners evicting under (a)(11) should re-evaluate the circumstances after the temporary relocation notice would expire, and see if any for-fault evict-ion grounds would apply for a follow up notice. Examples of potentially applicable grounds include nuisance and interference with property use under Rent Ordinance, Section 37.9(a)(3), and denial of access under 37.9(a)(6), depending on tenant's conduct.

The follow up notice may not be issued under 37.9(a)(2), from which this conduct is expressly exempt: "[t]he tenant has violated a lawful obligation or covenant of tenancy **other than** the obligation to surren-der possession upon proper notice.[356]"

R. Timing issues.

Length of the time before notice expires. Non-fault eviction notices are issued for periods of time significantly lengthier than most of their for-fault cousins. Majority of the notices are at least 30-60 days long, based on CC §§ 1946 and 1946.1, and many are extended even for longer time.[357] A notice can be given "at any time,[358]" meaning it can be given mid-month to terminate a month-to-month tenancy, but with the minimum amount of time provided before termination (30/60 days). "If agreed upon," a rare situation for San Francisco tenancies, the notice can be given not less than seven days before the expiration of the term thereof.[359] The core rule is that the notice has to be unequivocal, generally in instructing the recipient on what to do, and specifically not confusing about the timing.[127]

Section 8 and other government subsidized tenancies require a minimum of 90 days for the notice.[360]

Timing issues with the relocation assistance payments. Prompt offering of the compensation is important and may otherwise invalidate the notice when not complied with. For many of the non-fault notices, initial portions of the relocation assistance fees are due on or before the service of the notice.[361] Those tenants who may claim the protected status (in eviction causes where applicable) also have to do it timely, or risk the status being waived.[362] The same is true for tenants' claims for additional relocation payments due to a disability or for a household with children, although the timing of handling disability claims is not as stringent.[363]

S. Compensation to tenants.

Majority of the non-fault evictions have a common element that all for-fault evictions lack: some kind of a compensation for the tenants being evicted. How exactly tenants are compensated depends on the kind of the eviction ground deployed (and, in the case of the "Good Samaritan" cause, the tenancy itself is the prize), but the compensation requirement is almost in every other cause.

Regulations regarding tenant compensation change often. Most rates are re-indexed annually. For the payments established by the Rent Board, new rates are usually announced at the end of January, to commence on the first day of March. Additionally, new rules on compensation are frequently proposed and almost as frequently enacted, possibly several times in the course of a year. Changes are usually in the direction of increasing the awards, but not always.[364] Practitioners are strongly advised to check for latest rates from the applicable legislative sources (depending on the particular eviction cause), before issuing a notice.

Additional compensation due to a disability claim, or for the households with children, may only materialize if requested by tenants.[365]

The most common relocation assistance regulation is spelled out under Section 37.9C. It applies to six types of non-fault evictions: 37.9(a)(8)(i), (a)(8)(ii), (a)(10), (a)(11) [when over 20 days], and (a)(12).[366] Since the issuance of most non-fault notices involves significant amounts paid to tenants at the time the notice is served, it is important to recognize the financial risks involved. Consider the following two, under 37.9C: first, if the notice is later rescinded, only a reissuance of the same kind of notice, and only within 180 days from service of the initial notice, will allow a landlord to rely on the compensation previously tendered to the tenant;[367] and, second, "payment or acceptance of relocation expenses shall not operate as a waiver of any rights a tenant may have under law.[368]"

Almost all other evictions have their own compensation provisions: an Ellis Act eviction [(a)(13)] is separately covered by Section 37.9A;[369] for the condo-conversion [(a)(9)], see S.F. Subdivision Code, Sections 1392, 1393; for the lead remediation and abatement of lead poisoning, or of "nuisances" under S.F. Health Code, Article 11 [(a)(14)], see S.F. Admin. Code, Chapter 72, or CC § 1947.9, if relocation is less than for 20 days. A demolition eviction under (a)(10) may be either subject to the relocation assistance payable per Section 37.9C or per 37.9A(f).[370] It appears though that the removal of units per development agreements [(a)(15),

S.F. Admin. Code, Chapter 56] does not necessarily provide for a compensation payment.[371]

Status of eligibility to payments under 37.9C is covered below, as one common to several types of no-fault evictions. Other compensation mechanisms are explained under their respective eviction types, those being unique to those particular kinds of notices.

(i) Notice For Not Eligible Tenants.

If the occupants are not authorized tenants, a shorter eviction notice may be available to the landlord under Section 37.9(a)(7) [See, ¶ II (9)].

If the occupants are authorized, but aren't "eligible tenants," the eviction notice is still required, possibly for a shorter period of time: it will be a 30-day notice (since the occupancy is less than a year, under CC §§ 1946, 1946.1), and will not provide for otherwise required payments under Section 37.9C(b) and (e). Note that the payment requirements of Section 37.9C are "in addition[372]" to all other rights tenants may have, hence we say it is only a "possibly" shorter period. Other requirements may demand an extension, such a 90-day or longer notice for HUD-regulated tenancies.

(ii) Notice For Eligible Tenants.

Notice of available compensation for eligible tenants contains signifycantly more information, mainly covering two topics: payments and the tenants' right to claim a protected status.

A tenant thus may be simply "eligible" for the main payment, or also "be entitled to receive an additional payment" for the age, disability, or being having a child under 18 y.o. in the household,[373] and yet may or may not gain a right to claim protected status, based on the years in residency.

Notice to "eligible tenants" suggests that occupants were authorized by the landlord, and are residing at the subject property "for 12 or more months." Section 37.9C(a)(2). For the length of the notice, CC § 1946.1(c) allows for a 30-day notice if the residency is "for less than one year." Since 12 months and one year appear to be synonymous periods,[374] it follows that the OMI notice to eligible tenants will be a 60-day notice, and it will include additional disclosures for the payments due.

The idea that a moving-in landlord has to pay a relocation fee for vacating tenants is not obvious, it was added to the ordinance in 2006.

San Francisco present payment requirement was held to be lawful and constitutional at its current level,[375] while City's attempts to substantially increase those amounts were found unconstitutional and "unreasonable.[376]"

The Rent Board establishes required payment amounts and updates them annually.[377] For the terminations under Section 37.9C, in March 2019 through February 2020 period, a relocation amount per tenant is established at $6,980.00, with the maximum amount due per unit at $20,939.00 [this time it is off by $1 from the tripled amount of a per-capita payment], plus additional $4,654.00 for each disabled or elderly (over 60 years old) tenant, and a household with minor children. [Board's Form 579] For relocation rates under the Ellis Act, see Form 578, or see joint Form 577 for all rates in one document.

T. Vacancy decontrol.

For-fault evictions usually leave no lasting mark on the property. By contrast, most non-fault evictions may affect the property and limit property owner's rights, including an ability to do a condo-conversion,[378] or rent at a market-level rent,[379] or rent at all, except to the original occupants or at the prior rent level, before certain time after the eviction expires.[380]

The above noted regulations are local mechanisms to compel offering vacated units at rates lower than the market level. The state counterpart statute is currently inactive, until and unless the Costa-Hawkins Act is repealed.[381] Relevant articles of the Costa-Hawkins Act for the vacancy decontrol are CC §§ 1954.52, 1954.53, and 1954.535, the latter covering government-subsidized tenancies and requiring a longer, "at least 90 days' written notice."

U. Statement Of Lawful Rent Due.

Lawful amount of rent due shall be stated in the notices issued under Sections 37.9(a)(8), (a)(9), (a)(10), (a)(11), and (a)(14).[382] When an eviction under those Sections involves termination of a government-subsidized tenancy, or where the subsidy contract is terminated or not renewed, "the landlord shall, within 10 days after giving the notice of termination of the program to the tenant, notify the Board in writing of the monthly rent the tenant was paying and the monthly rent paid by the program to the landlord on behalf of the tenant when the landlord gave notice to the tenant, and provide a copy of the notice to the Board to the tenant.[383]"

This is another significant difference between non-fault and for-fault notices, which lies in the fact that tenants have to keep paying rent until they vacate due to a non-fault notice. Acceptance of rent payments tendered during pendency of non-fault notices should not be seen as a waiver, which contrasts with the for-fault scenarios, where landlord's acceptance of rent may be argued as landlord's waiver of the "fault." (¶ II(1)(g)).

Nuances still may exist when the period for a non-fault notice ends earlier than a full month, yet the payment was made for a full month and accepted as such. Tenants argue that, by such payment, landlord accepts rent for the time after the notice has expired. Landlords in turn cite a rule that landlord's entitlement for the entire period of rent becomes due on the first day of that period.[384]

Don't overlook that the requirement of stating the rent amount is for the *lawful* rent amount. This qualifier has its own independent and important meaning. With certain exceptions, such as tenancies in the newer and unregulated units and tenancies in single-family residencies, the Ordinance regulates permissible rent increases in majority of tenancies in San Francisco.[385] And some of the tenancies are further regulated by other government subsidy programs, such as the HUD programs by the SFHA.[386] For those regulated tenancies, only the rent increases compliant with those regulations are "lawful." It follows that the currently charged amount has to be in compliance with both the substantive rules and regulations, and the procedural requirements for noticing the rent increase.[387]

V. Landlord's contact information, mandatory for no-fault notices.

Stating landlord's contact information is always preferable, regardless of the eviction type, as it had been pointed out in the earlier chapter (¶ II(2)(d)). What is a welcomed option for most of the for-fault notices (only mandatory for a non-payment of rent), is also a mandatory requirement in the non-fault scenarios.

Several instructions are expected to be given to the recipients of non-fault eviction notices. The recipients need to know when and how to inform a landlord about a potential "protected" status (relevant in OMI/RMI evictions), how to claim an additional relocation assistance under 37.9A or 37.9C, how to demand a walk-through inspection under CC

§ 1950.5, and, in most cases, how much, where, and to whom pay rent while still residing at the rental unit (see *e.g.* 37.9(c), first sentence),[382] and how to inform the landlord about their new or temporary location. All these instructions are typically made part of the non-fault eviction notice.

W. Statement regarding abandoned personal property.

Effective January 1, 2013, a statement regarding tenant's abandonment of personal property, optional in other situations, is expressly required for notices given under CC §§ 1946, 1946.1, as stated in the current version of the statute.

X. Service on subtenants and other occupants.

Generally, a CC § 1946 notice is required to be served only on the tenants mentioned in the lease.[251] In the light of the San Francisco local treatment of subsequent occupants (Rules 6.15A–E), it is prudent to include in the notice all known occupants by name, covering a potential argument that some later occupant became a lawful and entitled resident of the rental unit. Include also a general descriptor, something like "... and all other tenants, subtenants, and occupants in a form of tenancy unknown, claiming to have a right to possess the premises."

Caution has to be exercised here on two accounts. First, while all known residents should be mentioned in the notice, it does not always follow that all such residents receive the same treatment under the notice. For example, some of the residents may be "eligible" for relocation assistance while some not.[388]

Second, the notice itself may be deemed a communication from a landlord to an occupant, thus potentially triggering a change of status of such occupants via express acknowledgment of them by name, under Rules 6.15A–E, especially if this particular notice is later withdrawn, or the eviction not completed for any reason. Whenever the status of any named occupant is unknown or uncertain, include a disclaimer, along the lines that: "notifying any individuals in this notice by name does not change the status of such individuals as unauthorized occupants, subtenants, or replacement tenants, and may not be deemed as a waiver of the applicable property owner's rights or as a recharacterization of such occupants as subtenants, or as replacement tenants or original tenants. For any persons, other than those named on the lease or previously and separately authorized by the landlord, the notice shall not be deemed as acceptance or authorization of any individuals mentioned in this notice as approved co-tenants, subtenants, or in any way or form authorized residents of the subject property, or as a waiver of any rights, all rights being reserved."

The eviction notice does not change the terms of the tenancy and should not to be confused with the notice given under CC § 827.[92]

Y. Disclosures for the protected status of a household with a child, or an "educator."

Tenant's "protected" status went through a significant up-and-down cycle over this particular ordinance amendment (dubbed "the educators") from its enactment and in 2016, through a 2018 reversal of that ban, in full. First, effective May 23, 2016, the right previously recognized only for OMI and RMI evictions, was expanded to almost all non-fault eviction causes,[389] then the new ordinance was challenged in court, and the court enjoined the city from enforcing it, then the City appealed the decision and on February 14, 2018, it was reversed in full.[390]

The ordinance provision amends S.F. Admin. Code, Section 37.9(j).

The right to claim a child-related protection was given to a household with "a child under age 18 … resides in the unit, whereas the child … is a tenant in the unit or has a custodial or family relationship with a tenant in the unit, the tenant has resided in the unit for 12 months or more, and the effective date of termination of tenancy falls during the school year.[391]"

Same Ordinance 55-16 introduced a brand-new additional type of a potentially "protected" tenant status, dubbed the "educator.[392]" The constitutionality of this "educator" exception is doubtful, yet it is currently the law.

The "educator" definition included: "any person who works at a school in San Francisco as an employee or independent contractor of the school or of the governing body that has jurisdiction over the school, including, without limitation, all teachers, classroom aides, administrators, administrative staff, counselors, social workers, psychologists, school nurses, speech pathologists, custodians, security guards, cafeteria workers, community relations specialists, child welfare and attendance liaisons, and learning support consultants.[392]"

This definition of the tenant's "protected" status (eligibility to avoid an eviction), shall not be confused with the certain categories of tenants' eligibility for relocation payments. Definitions of tenants who are eligible for relocation assistance payments are applicable to almost all non-fault evictions. See, Sections 37.9A(e) and 37.9C(a), covered in ¶ III (S), above, and more under each specific non-fault ground. To illustrate the differences in two "status" concepts, consider that someone who is over 60 years of age and who lived on the property for 4 years *will* be eligible for an additional payment, but will *not* be able to claim protective status based on age, and will still have to vacate, albeit with an additional payment in hand.

There is also a procedural difference in claiming the statuses: the "protection" from an eviction has to be stated within 30 days or deemed waived,[393] while claiming eligibility for an additional payment has no strict deadline or waiver procedure, can be claimed as late as 15 days before the expiration of the notice.[394]

There are only two exceptions under the revised version of Section 37.9(j): "where there is only one rental unit owned by the landlord in the building, or where the owner who will move into the unit pursuant to a Section 37.9(a)(8) eviction has a custodial or family relationship with a child under the age of 18 who will reside in the unit with the owner.[395]" Logically, this protection also would not apply when an eviction is timed so that the expiration of the notice falls in between the school years.[396]

In addition to the right to claim "protected" status for households with children under Section 37.9(j), a tenant has a right to claim protected status due to age or disability, under Section 37.9(i). The later protection is addressed below, under an OMI eviction, Section III (10), and applies to an RMI eviction as well.

Z. Anti-Merger Prohibitions.

Any eviction performed under the Rent Ordinance, if successful, results in recovery of some previously occupied residency. The recovered space may be a part of a larger property, and may be deemed "merged" into that property. A merger is often an unobvious result of that eviction, and is therefore dangerous. Demolition scenarios are much easier to recognize in comparison to the mergers, and there are, in fact, just grounds allowing eviction for that exact purpose.[397]

Currently, merging residential units is generally prohibited, subject to some exceptions.[398] This affects most of the non-fault evictions, (a)(8) through (a)(14), even though a recent appellate decision found a local ordinance prohibiting merger for 10 years following a non-fault eviction preempted by state law.[399] Similar prohibition still may apply not only to mergers, but also to the removal/demolishing or such units, or reducing more than 25% of their original floor area, or converting them to non-residential use or "student housing." *Id.*, S.F. Planning Code, Sec. 317. Merger regulations change often, and the practitioners are advised to check the applicable rules for an updated version immediately before issuing the notice.

The San Francisco Planning Department provides for a step-by-step procedure to apply for and obtain a merger or demolition permit.[400]

The issue with merger often comes up when a single-family house, where the owner recovers possession to the downstairs ("in-law") unit. In the case when an upstairs unit is vacant, or occupied by the owner, the owner may intentionally or accidentally merge the downstairs into the main living area upstairs. Is this truly a merger? It may be deemed as such. Under the Rent Ordinance, an in-law unit is considered a separate unit.[401] It is also within the S.F. Planning Code's definition of an "unauthorized unit,[402]" demolition or merger of which is generally prohibited, unless expressly permitted.[403] A more difficult situation to argue, but still possible, is a situation where the single-room-occupancy "SRO" units are merged as a result of an eviction.

It is therefore vitally important for the issuer of an non-fault eviction notice under grounds (a)(8) through (a)(14) to ensure that the recovery of the aimed-at residency will not result in merging it with another unit, unless there is an exception, or a valid permit allowing to proceed.

With these common characteristics of the non-fault notices being covered, now let us turn to the specifics of the notices, issued for the particular "just cause" non-fault grounds.

10. Owner moving in ("OMI"). SFRO § 37.9(a)(8)(i).

(a) Type and Length of the Notice: either 30- or 60-day notice, depending on whether the subject tenancy is for less or more than one year, per CC §§ 1946, 1946.1; 90-day notice in cases where this eviction involves termination of a government-subsidized tenancy. Rent Ordinance coverage for this type of eviction includes S.F. Admin Code, Sections 37.3(d), 37.3(f), 37.9(a)(8), 37.9(c), 37.9(i), 37.9(j), 37.9B, 37.9C, and Rule 12.14.

(b) When applicable. This type of eviction is used when the landlords recover possession of a rental unit for their own personal occupancy. It has been held that property owners have a constitutional right to reclaim real property for personal use.[404] Issuance of this notice is applicable when "[t]he landlord seeks to recover possession in good faith, without ulterior reasons and with honest intent ... [f]or the landlords use or occupancy as his or her principal residence for a period of at least 36 continuous months.[405]"

(c) Notice Requirements.

(i) Under Section 37.9B.

Several general notice requirements apply to this type of notice, see ¶ I and ¶ III (P)—(Y), above. In addition to the previously discussed, specific disclosures are required, as spelled out in Section 37.9B(c)(1)–(7):

"(1) The identity and percentage of ownership of all persons holding a full or partial percentage ownership in the property;

(2) The dates the percentages of ownership were recorded;

(3) The name(s) of the landlord endeavoring to recover possession and, if applicable, the names(s) and relationship of the relative(s) for whom possession is being sought and a description of the current residence of the landlord or relative(s);

(4) A description of all residential properties owned, in whole or in part, by the landlord and, if applicable, a description of all residential properties owned, in whole or in part, by the landlord's grandparent, parent, child, grandchild, brother, or sister for whom possession is being sought;

(5) The current rent for the unit and a statement that the tenant has the right to re-rent the unit at the same rent, as adjusted by Section 37.9B(a) ...;

(6) The contents of Section 37.9B, by providing a copy of same; and

(7) The right the tenant(s) may have to relocation costs and the amount of those relocation costs."

Most of these requirements are self-explanatory, but for some a clarification seems necessary. It is offered here under the same numbering order as used in Section 37.9B(c).

(1) Identity of the persons holding ownership in the property is not an obvious concept, when you consider that the term "person" includes entities.[406] In the context of an owner- or relative-move-in eviction, it seems logical to consider only the natural persons, the individuals, as moving-in persons, for many reasons, including that this is an eviction for a purpose of residency and of a residential unit. Although any entity may establish its residency-office or headquarters,[407] it had been said by Sir Edward Coke, that corporations have no soul,[408] and thus may not be equaled with a physical individual for the purposes of unit's residential use. The requirement for the evictor to be a natural person is enforced by Rule 12.14(a).

Trusts appear to be the only exception to the entity rule, when the trustees are individuals, since the legal title to the property of the trusts is held by its trustees, especially when such individual-trustees are also beneficiaries of same trusts, and when they are granted powers to administer the title.[409] Such trustees may then have a right to take possession of the property, and the required authority to initiate an eviction.[410]

In the case of a fractional or shared co-ownership, this individual vs. entity limitation only applies to the co-owners intending to occupy the property. A portion of the same property can still be owned by an entity, and it won't trump the eviction, if properly disclosed and when the individual co-owner is the one who moves in.

There can only be one owner to exercise an OMI eviction, even if the property is owned by several owners and has multiple units. On the other hand, there can be unlimited amount of relatives to move-in under an RMI eviction, provided that their related owner resides at the property, there is no restriction on the amount of relatives stated in the Ordinance.[411]

(4) The requirement under 37.9B(c)(4) to disclose *all* owned residential properties does not limit the scope of disclosure to the properties owned in San Francisco, the state, or the country. Nor does it exclude non-vacant or part-owned properties. Consider that even a timeshare property technically needs to be disclosed under this requirement, since it is a property, which the owner has a right to occupy, albeit only for a limited time per year.[412]

A 2017 San Francisco case *Azar v. Rodriguez* established that the definition of a "landlord" for this requirement of property disclosure includes co-owners' other real property, even if those co-owners are not ones moving in.[413]

This disclosure of owned properties requirement is independent from offering vacant properties for relocation. Those properties have to be disclosed too—it means that the unavailable owned property is disclosed once, while a vacant property gets to be mentioned twice in the same notice. An interesting detail is in determining whether the vacant property is a comparable rental unit. If the vacant unit is comparable, the notice is either not issued, or withdrawn when such unit becomes available during the pendency term of the notice.[414] Only if a non-comparable unit is available, the eviction may proceed.

A non-comparable vacant rental unit shall be disclosed in the notice and offered to the being-evicted tenants[414] at that unit's current market level rent—it had been adjudged that for an ordinance to cap or regulate the level of rent a landlord can ask for a replacement unit would run in conflict with the Costa-Hawkins Act.[415]

If a non-comparable vacant unit is in the same multi-unit building, and the tenant is unprotected,[416] the eviction may proceed the same way as if all other units were vacant, just make sure that the vacant units were disclosed in the notice.

But if a non-comparable vacant unit is in the same building, and the tenant *is* protected, the eviction may only proceed when the necessary conditions are present. See, ¶ III(Y) [children and "educators"] and ¶ III(10)(d)(ii) [age/disability].

Determining whether the vacant unit is "comparable" is not obvious.

After all, each real property is unique.[17] In the case *Bakanauskas v. Urdan*, it was noted that, in a context of an owner move-in eviction, owner's own subjective factors of desirability of a particular unit must be considered, or the rent ordinance would be "unsatisfactory confiscatory.[417]" Court in *Bakanauskas* considered factors of noise, light, views, location, and even available closets as factors making two otherwise similar apartments not comparable. The court also held that, even if the unit subject to eviction is inferior to the other vacant unit, it only further confirms units being not comparable, but does not bar an eviction. *Id*. at 628.

(6) Attaching copies of the ordinance sections. A copy of Section 37.9B must always be attached.[418] A copy of Section 37.9C must also be attached.[419] Attaching a copy of Section 37.9(a)(8) is not expressly required, but it won't hurt to include. For eligible tenants, I also include the disclosure form for the minimally required payment amounts. The Rent Board issues and updates this form and makes it available for download in English and other languages.[420]

A reason to include the copy of Section 37.9(a)(8) is to make a working reference to the statute. There are plenty of required disclosures to be made in the notice; those not expressly required can still be made by referencing the underlying ordinance.[421]

What copy to use for the notice attachment? This author's personal opinion was that it should be the version maintained by the code's official publisher, the American Legal Publishing Corp., the "amlegal.com." It is *not* the opinion of the San Francisco Housing Court, which finds notices with amlegal attachments defective.[422] Until the issue is clarified further by either the courts or legislation, the approach seems to be to use the copy published by the Rent Board itself.[34] The versions do differ. For example the amlegal publication does not include commentaries, inserted in [ ] brackets in the Board's version.

(7) Tenants' right to relocation costs directly depends on their eligibility status. (¶ III (S)). If the subject notice is issued to tenants ineligible for payments (¶ III (S)(i)), the disclosure about the payment entitlement under 37.9B(c)(7) should still be made and address the non-eligibility for payment pursuant 37.9C(a)(2).

Naturally, all notice disclosures covered above are also applicable for a notice issued to "eligible tenants," whose status is defined in Section

37.9C(a)(2). Since there are additional disclosures required to be made in a notice for eligible tenants, an important step for the notice drafter is to determine tenant's eligibility. See above, ¶ III (S) (i) and (ii).

(ii) Under Rule 12.14.

It would be too easy if all requirements for this notice were named in a single unified list. But don't worry, the OMI notice is not in danger of being a boring checklist exercise. Now that we have covered the general elements, and the necessary disclosures under 37.9B, here are the elements required by the Rule 12.14(a)–(d):

12.14(a) mandates the landlord to be a natural person or a group of natural persons. Necessity and logic of this requirement is covered above, under ¶ III (10)(c)(i)(1). Reading Sec. 37.9(a)(8)(i) together with Rule 12.14(a) brings me to a conclusion that this definition is concerned with the moving-in landlord, rather than to require that every co-owner of the building to be an individual (*i.e.* unrelated share of interest in the property title can be vested in an entity). As for the RMI evictions, this appears to be a non-issue since it would impossible to be a relative of an entity, unless there are some complex trust issues, and the moving-in person is a relative of a trustee or a beneficiary.

Same Rule 12.14(a) also requires the subject landlord to hold at least 10% interest in the property, if such interest was recorded before February 21, 1991, or 25% for any interest recorded or changed later.[423] The interest can be combined, including by the moving-in domestic partners.[424] This concept is not always obvious and has several sub-issues in itself:

[1] Transfer of interest. The required share of interest can be obtained before issuance of notice by an obvious solution—transfer of necessary amount of interest in the property. This transaction should always be considered when the granting holder is an entity, to transfer to a natural person, to satisfy Rule 12.14(a). Parties should not transfer without first consulting with a tax specialist, because the change in ownership may trigger consequent tax obligations, a corresponding reassessment in property tax, and may also require to pay a transfer tax, sometimes a significant sum.[425]

[2] Fractional ownership. A title to real property may be held by multiple co-owners, under several recognized forms of fractional ownership. Most often scenario is when the property is co-owned by "tenants

in common" or "TIC." A co-owner, or an owner of a fractional interest in property can exercise her rights and perform an OMI eviction. See, e.g., *Bakanauskas v. Urdan*.[417]

This is especially so, when the TIC co-owners enter into an exclusive-use or exclusive right of occupancy TIC agreements ("ERO"). There was once an attempt to discourage the TIC/ERO practice in San Francisco on the level of a municipal ordinance in San Francisco. That ordinance was found unconstitutional in 2004.[426]

[3] Transfer of units. Several considerations have to be taken into account when any rental unit is transferred (either sold to a new owner or exchanged between existing co-owners). Although an owner of a real property is usually free to dispose of it, the fact of transferring ownership rights does not affect the requirements and prohibitions under the OMI/RMI provision, namely that a certain unit is either occupied by the then-evicting owner or such owner's relative for 36 months, or not rented in violation of the Ordinance for the first 5 years following the eviction. In other words, if Owner A moved-in under an OMI notice, and then sold the unit to Owner B next month, Owner A either remains to reside at the place, or the place is offered back at the previous rent rate[427] and to the previous tenant.[428] If the same sale takes place after Owner A lived on-site for 36 months, there is no longer a requirement for Owner A to stay, but the place can't be rented at market rent for two more years.

Transfer of a unit may also be relevant to establishing the residence of an evicting "owner." While there can be unlimited amount of relatives moving-in under an RMI eviction, there can be but one "owner's unit" for the purposes of an OMI eviction.[429] An owner may petition the Rent Board to change the designated unit, based on hardship or disability. (*Id.*)

12.14(b), effective January 1, 2018, contains 11 requirements of what items to include with the notice.[430] First seven match those under Section 37.9B(c)(1)–(7).

The additional requirements of what to include with the notice are:

> "(8) a declaration executed by the landlord under penalty of perjury stating:
> (i) the reason why the landlord or relative is moving from his/her current residence to the unit for which possession is

being sought;

(ii) that the landlord seeks to recover possession of the unit in good faith, without ulterior reasons and with honest intent, for use or occupancy as the principal residence of the landlord or the landlord's relative (identified by name and relation to the landlord), for a period of at least 36 continuous months, as set forth in Ordinance Sections 37.9(a)(8)(i) and (ii);

(iii) whether the landlord served a notice to vacate pursuant to Ordinance Section 37.9(a)(8) for a different unit; and,

(iv) whether the landlord has recovered possession of other rental units in the City and County of San Francisco for any reason under Ordinance Section 37.9(a) other than nonpayment of rent in which the tenant displaced from such rental unit had resided for at least 36 consecutive months;

(9) a warning that the tenant must submit a statement to the landlord within 30 days of service of the notice to vacate, with supporting evidence, if the tenant claims to be a member of a protected class under Ordinance Sections 37.9(i) or (j), and that failure to do so shall be deemed an admission that the tenant is not protected by Sections 37.9(i) or (j);

(10) a form[431] prepared by the Rent Board stating that a tenant's failure to timely act in response to a notice to vacate may result in a lawsuit by the landlord to evict the tenant, that advice regarding the notice to vacate is available from the Rent Board, and that the tenant may be eligible for affordable housing programs through the Mayor's Office of Housing and Community Development; and

(11) a blank change of address form[432] prepared by the Rent Board that the tenant can use to keep the Rent Board apprised of any future change of address."

Requirements stated under Rule 12.14(c)–(f) are not about additional disclosures to be made in the notice. Subsections (c) through (e) provide relevant definitions, and (f) covers a requirement of filing of the Statement of Occupancy after the service of notice.

12.14(c) explains that there can only be one "principal place of residence" and how to prove a particular place;

12.14(d) provides for the disability standard: "if the tenant meets the standard for blindness or disability under the federal Supplemental Security Income/California State Supplemental Program." This definition, although wide in its coverage, is still narrower than one under which tenant's eligibility for an additional payment is established, where the tenant is "disabled within the meaning of Section 12955.3 of the California Government Code.[433]" The Rent Board provides for a hearing procedure, when a landlord elects to challenge tenant's claimed disability in the OMI/RMI eviction. Landlord's right to challenge tenant's claimed protected status is reflected in Sections 37.9(i)(4) and 37.9(j)(3). There is currently no generally applicable hearing procedure, if the disability is challenged in evictions under other just causes.

12.14(e) suggests a non-exclusive list of what evidence can be considered in finding for landlord's lack of good faith.

12.14(f), similarly to Section 37.9(a)(8)(vii), requires the evicting landlord to keep the Rent Board informed about the status of recovery of the subject rental unit, and landlord's or his/her relative consequent occupancy of the same.[434] This information is provided on one of the three variations of Form 546 (A, B, or C), depending on the applicable scenario: the unit is still not recovered[435]; the unit is recovered and occupied by the landlord/relative[436]; or the unit is recovered and no longer occupied by the landlord/relative.[437]

(d) Tenant's Right To Claim A Protected Status.

In addition to the disclosures covered above, the eviction notice for owner/ relative move-in must inform a tenant of the restrictions in Ordinance Sections 37.9(i) and 37.9(j).[438] Landlord's request for tenant's information is made in writing.[439] Sub-sections (i) and (j) cover instances when tenants are protected against this kind of eviction and when those protections do not apply.

Tenants receiving an OMI notice must be informed about protections available for aged or disabled tenants, for the "educators," and for the tenancies with minor children, and that those tenants to whom those protections apply, must advise the landlord in writing within 30 days if the tenant is claiming a "protected status" under Section 37.9(i) or 37.9(j). If a tenant fails to claim protected status due to the age/ disability within 30 days following service of the notice, the status is deemed waived.[440] Similar requirement exists for claiming protection per Section 37.9(j).[441] Child- and "educator"-related protections are covered in Section ¶ III (Y), as they are available to several types of non-fault evictions.

Disability- and age-related protections are specific for the OMI and RMI evictions. With the passage of time, certain tenants obtain a right to claim "protected" status, meaning that they may not be evicted under OMI and RMI "non-fault" causes of eviction.[442] As mentioned previously, the tenants obtain a *right* to claim their "protected" status, rather than the status itself—that status has to be timely and properly claimed when the landlord makes an inquiry, or the tenant risks to waive it.[440]

Tenant's protected status can be challenged and determined by the Rent Board.[443] The question of status is brought up in two situations: a tenant affirmatively claims it in a Tenant Estoppel Certificate,[444] usually made a part of the disclosures provided to a buyer at property sale, or a tenant claims it in response to an owner- or a relative-move-in eviction notice. For the purposes of an eviction, the claim, together with supporting evidence, has to be presented "[w]ithin 30 days of personal service by the landlord of a written request," or the eviction notice,[443] thus the claims made in the Estoppel Certificate often do not apply, and tenants risk to waive their rights, if the status is not reclaimed within 30 days following the service of notice.

With regard to confirming or contesting the tenant's status, an appropriate route is to start at the administrative level of the Rent Board, rather than by seeking judicial determination of such status in court.[445] If one of the parties is unsatisfied with the Rent Board finding and its consequent appeal, determination by court is then available.[446] Federal caselaw suggests that "[i]f a landlord is skeptical of a tenant's alleged disability or the landlord's ability to provide an accommodation, it is incumbent upon the landlord to request documentation or open a dialogue.[447]" For a detailed discussion of factors considered in establishing tenant's status at administrative level vs. seeking judicial determination, see the unpublished, but instructive 2017 decision in *200 Arguello Assocs., LLC v. Dyas.*[448]

(i) <u>Protected status under 37.9(i)</u>.

In addition to the protections available under Section 37.9(j) (children and "educators," covered in ¶ III (Y)), OMI- and RMI-specific protections due to tenants' age and disability are available.

There are three defined types of tenants' "protected" status under

Section 37.9(i):

(1) Tenant who is "60 years of age or older and has been residing in the unit for 10 years or more[449]";

(2) Tenant who is disabled or blind "within the meaning of the federal Supplemental Security Income/California State Supplemental Program (SSI/SSP), and who is determined by SSI/SSP to qualify for that program or who satisfies such requirements through any other method of determination as approved by the Rent Board" "and has been residing in the unit for 10 years or more[450]";

(3) Tenant who "is catastrophically ill," meaning who is disabled as defined in the category above "and who is suffering from a life threatening illness as certified by his or her primary care physician" and "has been residing in the unit for five years or more.[451]"

(ii) Exemptions to protections under 37.9(i).

There are three kinds of exemptions, under which the eviction may still go forward. An OMI/RMI eviction may still proceed over the tenant's claimed protected status, under any one of the following exempting scenarios:

- the subject unit is the only unit owned by the landlord in the building, or

- or all other units, besides the one where the landlord resides, are also occupied by tenants claiming any of 37.9(i) versions of the protected status; or

- the moving-in landlord or the "qualified relative" is over 60 years old.[452]

Note that the exemption for ownership of units all occupied by protected tenants may include ownership under a TIC agreement.[453] Also important to note that the requirement of the landlord's residency in the building *prior* to the eviction does not demand his residency to be in the unit the landlord owns.

(e) Other Requirements And Limitations For OMI Eviction.

Regardless of the OMI eviction's type, length, or tenant's eligibility or protective status, the following requirements apply:

(i) Landlord's Good Faith.

As it was covered under the generally required elements [¶ I (F)], acting in good faith is an obvious and general requirement for any type of eviction, but is especially requested in the non-fault evictions,[120] including the OMI, where it is expressly and extensively codified, effective January 1, 2018.[454] On the state-level, the landlord may be ordered "to pay treble the amount of any increase in rent which the tenant has paid," and other costs and fees, if an OMI/RMI eviction involved fraud in fulfilling the occupancy requirement.[455]

OMI-related suggestions of what may indicate landlord's acting in bad faith include:

"if a landlord times the service of the notice, or the filing of an action to recover possession, so as to avoid moving into a comparable unit, or to avoid offering a tenant a replacement unit.[456]";

"(1) the landlord has failed to file the notice to vacate with the Rent Board as required by Section 37.9(c), (2) the landlord or relative for whom the tenant was evicted did not move into the rental unit within three months after the landlord recovered possession and then occupy said unit as that person's principal residence for a minimum of 36 consecutive months, (3) the landlord or relative for whom the tenant was evicted lacks a legitimate, bona fide reason for not moving into the unit within three months after the recovery of possession and/or then occupying said unit as that person's principal residence for a minimum of 36 consecutive months, (4) the landlord did not file a statement of occupancy with the Rent Board as required by Section 37.9(a)(8)(vii), (5) the landlord violated Section 37.9B by renting the unit to a new tenant at a rent greater than that which would have been the rent had the tenant who had been required to vacate remained in continuous occupancy and the rental unit remained subject to this Chapter 37 ...[457]";

"(6) the landlord served a notice to vacate pursuant to Ordinance Section 37.9(a)(8) for a different unit and has not sought a rescission or withdrawal of that notice; (7) the landlord has recovered possession of multiple rental units in the same building within 180 days of the service of the notice to vacate pursuant to Ordinance Section 37.9(a)(8); and/or

(8) the landlord completed buyout negotiations as defined in Ordinance Section 37.9E(c) with any other tenant(s) in the building.[458]"

Findings of fact under the above listed categories raise a rebuttable presumption of bad faith.[459]

Other issues often raised in an argument of bad faith are: retaliation, if the move-out date is within 180 days from tenant's complaint, and timing an eviction in violation of the terms of an existing term of the lease, *e.g.* to terminate a lease sooner than the agreed-upon term expires.

Conversely, indicating to a tenant during buyout or settlement negotiations that the landlord would, unless the settlement is achieved, seek to evict under an owner-move-in ground, is not an indication of bad faith.[460]

(ii) Continuous occupancy for 36 months.

The language of this just cause for eviction says "at least 36 continuous months" in case of an OMI eviction, and the same requirement applies for an RMI. Even though the RMI eviction does not say "continuous,[461]" it would be a presumption of bad faith, if those 36 months were not "consecutive.[462]" Under the Oakland Ordinance, such presumption of violation of the ordinance was found being preempted, because it would conflict with the burden of proof requirements of Evidence Code, Section 500.[463]

Starting January 1, 2018, there is now a self-reporting requirement,[464] coupled with an administrative penalty "in the amount of $250 for the first violation, $500 for the second violation, and $1,000 for every subsequent violation.[465]" On the enforcement part, see also Sections 37.9(e) and (l).

Although there is now a requirement imposed on landlords to self-report, and also a statement that the Rent Board shall make reasonable efforts to notify displaced tenants,[466] tenants should still exercise own diligence in keeping their contact information updated and in discovering landlord's violation of the continuous occupancy rule, or risk their claim being barred as untimely.[467]

(iii) <u>The difference between the 3-year and 5-year rules</u>.

Aside from the occupancy requirement for 36 consecutive months, the unit may not be leased for rent "greater than the lawful rent in effect at the time the previous tenancy was terminated, plus any annual rent increases available under this Chapter 37," for next five years following the tenancy termination.[468] In practice, the difference between the two timing limitations is in the property's use: for the first three years, the property shall be occupied by the moving-in owner or relative, who won't be held as acting in bad faith, if she were to vacate after residing there for 36 months. Yet, if she does so vacate, the place may only be rented at its previous rent level, plus allowed increases, for two more years. And the place has to be offered to its prior tenant.[428]

Obviously, if the landlord does allow someone to rent the place prior to expiration of five years, and the new tenant occupies the place for more than 32 days, raising his rent beyond the previously allowed rate may only happen if the property is exempt from the rent control (*e.g.* a stand-alone single unit). However, if the unit would be considered rent-controlled, it will be prudent to wait out the entire five years before renting it out again.

(f) Validity of the notice at the time of issuance, and the requirement to update and follow up through recovery of possession.

Generally, a notice must be valid at the time it expires, not necessarily when it is issued.[235] However, in the case of an OMI notice, validity of its statements must be present at the time the notice is served.[469] This also applies to the relocation assistance fee, its first half being delivered on or before the service of the notice.[470] Even more, the notice is subject to an ongoing monitoring not only through the time it expires but until possession is recovered, including that through "any action filed," and thus the notice is required to be supplemented or withdrawn in case there is a change in availability of vacant units.[471]

(g) Other required elements.

Most of the common elements covered in the "Commonly Required Notice Elements" section of this book apply, such as: property descrip-tion [¶ I(A)], parties [¶ I(B)], date and signature [¶ I(H)], information about the Rent Board [¶ I(I)], notice of an option to request initial inspection [¶ I(K)], notice of abandoning personal property [¶ I(J)], notice given in other languages [¶ I(M)], optionally also including the statement whether this notice supersedes other notices [¶ I(G)]. The notice has to include a statement of the lawful rent due [¶ III(U)], and landlord or agent's contact information [¶ III(V)]. A copy of the notice with its proof of service has to be filed with the Rent Board.

(h) Section 8 application.

All the above-discussed requirements apply in the case of terminating a subsidized tenancy, in addition to any notice requirements by that subsidy program.[472]

An owner may terminate the subsidized tenancy for the "other good cause," which definition includes "[t]he owner's desire to use the unit for personal or family use, or for a purpose other than as a residential rental unit.[473]"

The notice shall be at least 90 days long, the tenants may not be obligated to pay more than their portion of rent during that 90-day period, the landlord will not be eligible to set an initial rent for five years following the date of termination, and the rate during those five years will remain the same as it was under the terminated subsidy program, plus the authorized increases under that subsidy program.[474]

As covered above in ¶ III (U) termination of a subsidized tenancy or the subsidy contract requires giving notice to Rent Board of what the tenant paid in rent and what was paid by the subsidy, and giving a copy of that notice to the tenant.[475]

11. Relative moving in ("RMI"). SFRO § 37.9(a)(8)(ii).

Requirements for the RMI notices are almost identical to those of the OMI notices, addressed at length immediately above.

Under an RMI notice, an owner can seek recovery of possession of a rental unit "[f]or the use or occupancy of the landlords grandparents, grandchildren, parents, children, brother or sister, or the landlords spouse or the spouses of such relations, as their principal place of residency for a period of at least 36 months ... For purposes of this Section 37.9(a)(8)(ii), the term spouse shall include Domestic Partners as defined in San Francisco Administrative Code Chapter 62.1 through 62.8.[476]"

There are three main points to distinguish in an RMI vs. an OMI eviction:

(1) For the RMI, an owner must either already reside at the subject property, or seek possession of a rental unit simultaneously with the relative for whom the RMI notice is issued.[476] Accordingly, RMI is not applicable to a single-unit rental property. This is not an obvious rule—consider that the Oakland Rent Ordinance is politely silent on the subject whether an owner needs to be a resident of the same building, where she desires to place her relatives.[477]

(2) Unlimited amount of relatives may move in. While there is only one "owner's unit" allowed in the building following an OMI eviction, there may exist many "relative's units" in that same building. The Rent Ordinance does not appear to limit the amount of relatives an owner is allowed to bring.

(3) The required statement of acting in good faith (S.F. Admin. Code, Sec. 37.9(a)(8), 1st sentence) still applies to the *landlord*, as opposed to the landlord's *relative*.[478] To err on the safe side, the owners should ensure that *both* the landlord and landlord's relative are pursuing this eviction in good faith and stating so in the notice.

12. Recovering possession for a sale in accordance with a condo-conversion. SFRO § 37.9(a)(9).

By way of a preamble, I start by observing that the conversion of residential units into condominiums in San Francisco is by itself a complicated topic, worthy of separate and detailed coverage going beyond this book's limits. Owners wishing to subdivide their property in this municipality have to see first if they can claim an exemption from the currently imposed moratorium on almost all conversions (an allowed municipal practice[479]), then to see if they can satisfy residency requirements, get their forms and building plans approved in multiple departments, get consent from all relevant neighbors and occupants. Overall, owners have to invest a lot of effort into the process with little to no prediction of success. As one court had said: "It should be noted that city approval of such conversions are extraordinarily difficult to obtain.[480]"

Regulating condo conversions at the city level has been confirmed as a proper and permissible process by a Rent Board, including when it is done retroactively;[481] and it has been generally deemed to be one of municipality's police powers.[482] Timing and order of the steps taken in a condo conversion are topics litigated often. Unlike the case with the OMI/RMI evictions, where reclaiming the property of personal use is seen warranted by the Constitution,[404] and further unlike the constitutional right of the property co-owners to enter into tenants-in-common ("TIC") agreements for an exclusive right to occupy a certain unit within a property,[483] or their constitutional right to choose between repairing and demolishing the property,[537] "the right to convert rental apartments to condominiums is not a fundamental constitutional right,[484]" at least until the owner receives a vested right in a form of a governmental promise or a building permit.[485]

But those efforts are not subject of this book. Here, we are exploring only one of the final chapters of that multilayered saga—the issuance of a notice for recovery of possession under the corresponding just cause, to sell the unit in accordance with the condo conversion, Section 37.9(a)(9). In comparison to the complexity of the condo-conversion process, the termination notice itself is quite simple and bears almost no special requirements.

(a) Prerequisite considerations; when this notice is applicable.

This just cause expressly refers to the "San Francisco subdivision ordinance,[486]" currently known as the "Subdivision Code of the City and County of San Francisco," S.F. Subd. Code, Section 1300, *et seq.*,[487] under which the residential unit is to be converted into a condominium, and to fall under the 37.9(a)(9) just cause for a corresponding eviction in order to sell the unit. To emphasize, it is not the condo-conversion itself, it the *sale* in accordance with that conversion is what gives an owner a ground to seek termination of a tenancy.[488]

Accordingly, all the steps and stages preceding the sale have to be successfully passed before the right for a notice under this ground may become available. See, S.F. Subdivision Code, Division 1. Those steps include submission of the application, obtaining a tentative map, and then a final map. As a condition for receiving the final map's approval, the applicant must demonstrate compliance with all applicable provisions of S.F. Housing, Building, Planning, and Subdivision Codes, and that the relevant violations were corrected or approved to be bonded-around.[489] Between the receipt of a tentative map and the approval of a final map, tenants must be notified of their right to purchase the unit, and must be offered units for sale after approval the final map and (typically for five or more units, currently halted on moratorium) the issuance of the Final Subdivision Public Report.[490] Besides those city-level requirements, the subdivider is to comply with the requirements for tenant notifications per California Government Code, some of which are overlapping.[491]

The packet submitted for the conversion application is expected to include the property's rental history.[492] The property's eviction and rent-increase history is considered as a potential ground to deny a tentative map issuance.[493]

If there were two or more non-fault evictions in the building, on separate units, since May 1, 2005, the conversion application would not be approved,[494] until ten years have passed since the last eviction.[495] If there was just one eviction, but the tenant was disabled or catastrophically ill, an application would not be approved,[496] and there is a more narrower 10-year rule to expunge that bar: one option for a 2-unit building, when owner-occupied for 10 years,[497] and another option for up to 6 units, also requiring ten years to pass, in this scenario "prior to registration for the lottery.[498]" Same 10-year bar applies to buyouts of tenants.[499]

As a note of curiosity, these 10-year bans on condo-conversion following buyouts were recently litigated and affirmed as constitutional,[500] while the similar 10-year bans on altering[501] and merging[502] units were both found conflicting with the Ellis Act and thus preempted. This might be attributed to Gov. Code, Section 7060.7(a), explaining that the legislative intent behind the Ellis Act was not to interfere with local governmental authority over regulation of condo conversions.[503] While the Ellis Act preempts local regulations over the question of an owner quitting the rental market (the ground for the above-mentioned decisions on striking 10-year ban on altering or merging units), the Map Act does not preempt local authority to regulate condo conversions.[504] It seems, however, Ellis Act's subsections 7060.7(b) and (c), could have been applied to the decisions on units' mergers and alterations, and yet they were not.

Additionally, non-fault evictions effectuated within seven years preceding the application have to be explained in satisfaction of requirements of Sections 1396(e)(3)(B)–(D).[505]

Within five days following the application, the first notice to tenants informing them about the proposed conversion is required to be given. "Said notice shall contain a description of the rights of tenants as herein provided, including the right of first refusal to purchase the unit,[506] the right to attend and be heard at the public hearing, the right to receive relocation assistance and benefits, the right of all tenants to extend occupancy for a period of from one to three years depending upon length of prior occupancy, the right of elderly and disabled tenants to a lifetime lease, and the prohibition against rent increases during the process of conversion.[507]" This notice is a continuous obligation on the owner-applicant, to be given to subsequent occupants, although the triggering timing on this follow-up is not clearly defined, creating a potential ambiguity.[508]

After the Final Map is recorded, the second notice goes out to tenants, informing them about their right to purchase the unit and extending the time for deciding on making a purchase for 60 days.[509] "All units approved for conversion shall be offered for sale to the tenants within one year of the issuance of the State Department of Real Estate's Final Sub-division Public Report.[510]"

(b) Type and Length of the Notice: Rent Ordinance coverage for this type of eviction includes S.F. Admin Code, Sections 37.3(d), 37.3(f) [with an exception for a bona-fide purchaser], 37.9(a)(9), 37.9(c), and 37.9(j). Notably, this type of termination is excluded from coverage for relocation payments under Section 37.9C.[511] Instead, the relocation compensation is covered by the S.F. Subdivision Code, Sections 1392 (moving expenses) and 1393 (relocation assistance).

The termination notice itself shall be no lesser than for 30 or 60 days, depending on whether the subject tenancy is for less or more than one year, per CC §§ 1946, 1946.1; 90 days in cases where this eviction involves termination of a government-subsidized tenancy after expiration of its initial term.[512]

While the notice may not be for a lesser period than stated above, it must follow 120 days for each tenant who did not exercise a right to purchase the unit,[513] for which tenants would have additional 60 days to contemplate on,[509] thus equaling to at least a 180-day period from the moment the Final Map is recorded preceding the termination notice.

(c) Notice Requirements.

Good faith is a generally required element in every notice. Specifically for this type of termination, see, *Pongputmong v. City of Santa Monica*,[514] not approving an otherwise deemed-approved condo-conversion application if tenants' consent was obtained through coercion or misrepresentation.

Moving expenses and relocation assistance under the S.F. Subdivision code are not made part of the termination notice. On one hand, the availability of those benefits expires with the 120-day period of exercising the tenant's options, preceding the termination notice,[515] on another hand, it may be extended with the lease renewal generally,[516] and is extended for tenants over 62 years old indefinitely.[517] It thus seems prudent from the practical standpoint, to include benefit-related disclosures in the notice.

Disclosures related to tenant's potential protected status are also to be part of the termination notice.

(d) Tenant's Right To Claim A Protected Status and other limitations.

Tenants' rights to rent- and eviction-control protections are generally not affected by a condo-conversion process, if the tenancy precedes the conversion.[518] I say "generally," because occasionally an unexpected loophole surfaces and even survives judicial review. In 2018, in Oakland, in a non-published decision, the court of appeal upheld a scheme, where one entity bought 4 recently converted condos in one building, formerly a fourplex with formerly four rent-controlled tenancies, and successfully raised rent in each apartment 125%.[519] This would appear running contrary to the 2019 published decision in *Chun v. Del Cid*, decided based on the LA ordinance, where it was held that the property's design does not control (there, a single-family residence), instead the controlling factor is the use (there, rented by nine separate locked rooms), thus treating the property as a rent-controlled multi-unit apartment building.[63]

Aside from the above comments, additional protections for the tenants under this eviction ground are available:

(i) Under the S.F. Subdivision Code.

Nonpurchasing tenants aged 62 or older get a right for a so-called "lifetime" lease. It is not exactly measured by the lifetime of the tenant, but rather extended to include a lifetime of an approved co-occupant, "related to the tenant by blood or marriage and is aged 62 or older at the time of death or demise of such tenant.[520]" A requirement for a lifetime lease was upheld as constitutional.[521]

Because the statutory language states that no subdivider should "refuse to renew or extend a rental agreement" (*Id.*) to such nonpurchasing tenant, it logically follows that informing a tenant about this right to claim the renewal or extension is prudent.

(ii) Under the Rent Ordinance (S.F. Admin. Code).

As addressed above, the notice must inform a tenant of the restrictions in Ordinance Section 37.9(j),[522] the protection for households with child(ren) and so-called "educators." Landlord's request for tenant's information is made in writing.[523] This ground does not provide for an all-time protected status, only requiring that the termination notice has to expire within the San Francisco School District's summer break.

The tenant to whom those protections apply must advise the landlord in writing within 30 days if the tenant is claiming a "protected status" under Section 37.9(j). If a tenant fails to claim protected status within 30 days following service of the notice, the status is deemed waived.[524] Child- and "educator"-related protections are covered in Section ¶ III (Y), as they are available to several types of non-fault evictions.

(iii) <u>Other limitations under decided precedents</u>.

If during the application for condo-conversion the owner makes any agreements or concessions, such agreements may be held enforceable even if the owner were later to abandon the conversion path and seek to terminate tenancies under the Ellis Act instead.[525] A similarly dangerous effect was reached in the case, where the conversion had been already achieved.[526] On the other hand, if the agreements or concessions were made solely between the co-owners, including the owners' agreement to convert to condominiums following the Ellis Act termination of tenancies, these agreements do not affect owners' right to proceed under the Ellis Act.[527]

(e) Other required elements.

Most of the common elements covered in the "Commonly Required Notice Elements" section of this book apply, such as: property description [¶ I(A)], parties [¶ I(B)], date and signature [¶ I(H)], information about the Rent Board [¶ I(I)], notice of an option to request initial inspection [¶ I(K)], notice of abandoning personal property [¶ I(J)], notice given in other languages [¶ I(M)], optionally also including the statement whether this notice supersedes other notices [¶ I(G)]. The notice has to include a statement of the lawful rent due [¶ III(U)], and landlord or agent's contact information [¶ III(V)]. A copy of the notice with its proof of service has to be filed with the Rent Board within 10 days from the service.

(f) Section 8 application.

All the above-discussed requirements apply in the case of terminating a subsidized tenancy, in addition to any notice requirements by that subsidy program.[528]

A. Volkov. Eviction Notice In San Francisco.

An owner may terminate the subsidized tenancy for the "other good cause," which definition includes "A business or economic reason for termination of the tenancy (such as sale of the property, renovation of the unit...)[529]"

The notice shall be at least 90 days long, the tenants may not be obligated to pay more than their portion of rent during that 90-day period, the landlord will not be eligible to set an initial rent for five years following the date of termination, and the rate during those five years will remain the same as it was under the terminated subsidy program, plus the authorized increases under that subsidy program.[530]

As covered above in ¶ III(U) termination of a subsidized tenancy or the subsidy contract requires giving notice to Rent Board of what the tenant paid in rent and what was paid by the subsidy, and giving a copy of that notice to the tenant.[531]

13. Recovering possession in order to demolish or to otherwise permanently remove the rental unit from housing use. SFRO § 37.9(a)(10).

(a) Type and Length of the Notice: either 30- or 60-day notice, depending on whether the subject tenancy is for less or more than one year, per CC §§ 1946, 1946.1; 90-day notice in cases where this eviction involves termination of a government-subsidized tenancy. Rent Ordinance coverage for this type of eviction includes S.F. Admin Code, Sections 37.3(d), 37.3(f), 37.9(a)(10), 37.9(c), 37.9(j), 37.9C (unless the demolition is of an unreinforced masonry building pursuant to Building Code Chapters 16B and 16C, then 37.9A(e)). Rule 12.19 applies if the unit is restored or returned to the housing use.

(b) When applicable. This type of eviction is used when the rental unit is permanently removed from its housing use, generally meaning a demolition of the unit, although mergers and conversion/change of use are also included in this ground. The outcome differs from a termination under the "Ellis Act" eviction under Sec. 37.9(a)(13), where (i) the unit is not removed from its overall housing use, but only removed from the *rental* residential use, (ii) the entire building is affected rather than one or few units, and, in the case of a demolition, (iii) the units can still be returned back to the ordinary rental use. However, the Ellis Act and this ground remain closely related, and the reasoning behind either of these two evictions is the same—a right to withdraw a unit from its residential rental use.[532] Similarities in these causes allowed the court in 2016 to strike a local ordinance for a 10-year ban on mergers, under the doctrine of preemption,[533] followed by striking in 2018 a 10-year ban on alterations.[534]

Still, and unlike the Ellis Act,[535] this type of tenancy termination has to pass the muster of compliance[536] with the City's General Plan and one of the eight policy priorities of the San Francisco Planning Code, Sec. 101.1 (b)(3): "[t]hat the City's supply of affordable housing be preserved and enhanced." This is because "prior to issuing a permit for any demolition, conversion or change of use ... the City shall find that the proposed project ... is consistent with the Priority Policies ... [and] with the General Plan." Sec. 101.1(e). More particularly, the demolition is addressed in Section 317 of the S.F. Planning Code, which is a very actively developing statute, with changes and amendments happening almost every year.

A. Volkov. Eviction Notice In San Francisco.

(c) Prerequisite steps and considerations.

    (i) <u>Notice to tenants and prospective tenants prior to applying for a permit.</u>

Cal. Civil Code Sec. 1940.6 requires a notice prior to applying for a demolition permit, and said notice is given not only to the current tenants, but to prospective tenants as well.

Notices for reclassification, approval of conditional use, or variance are posted per S.F. Planning Code, Secs. 306.8, 333. Review of permit applications and removal of a residential unit (either authorized or unauthorized) require notice per S.F. Planning Code, Sec. 311(b), including the change of use (§ 311(b)(1)), alteration or removal of over 75% of the residential unit's interior (§ 311(b)(2)), and a removal of a residential unit (§ 311(c)(2)). The Zoning Administrator will issue its own notice as well (§ 311(d)). The notice shall include in the package the items identified in Sec. 311(d)(7). While some notices under this code require only a 10-day notice, a permit application review is to take place at least 30 days after the notice per Sec. 311 is given. The affidavit under Building Code Sec. 106A.1(10) [addressed below] is also required to be served on all tenants in the building and posted in a conspicuous common area within the building for at least 15 days.

    (ii) <u>Obtaining all necessary permits.</u>

This eviction ground expressly includes the requirement that "all the necessary permits" need to be obtained "on or before the date upon which notice to vacate is given." (S.F. Admin. Code, Sec. 37.9(a)(10)). In order to obtain such permits, following the necessary notifications covered above, the property owners make an application and receive an approved permit, provided the satisfy the criteria of S.F. Planning Code Section 317, and all applicable requirements. At this time, the owners need not to wait until the time to appeal an already-issued permit expires, the termination notice can be given immediately following the permit issuance.

It is owner's constitutional right to choose to choose to repair or demolish the property, and if the owner so desires and acts promptly, even a city-ordered demolition can be avoided.[537] However, if its aligned with the owner's intent, demolition is logically allowed, when such it is so ordered by the court or the City.[538]

Outside of that green-light exemption, and given the policy considerations mentioned above, success in obtaining an underlying permit for merger, demolition, or change of use is not at all guaranteed. It requires City's determination of whether denial of such application for permit, or an alternative directive (*e.g.*, approving a legalization of an non-conforming unit rather than the removal of it), is appropriate, and it is based on numerous factors considered by the Planning Commission.[539]

With regard to the unauthorized units' removal, it worth noting that, effective January 1, 2016, removal of a kitchen, stove, or bathroom is presumed equaling removal of a dwelling unit, and requires an applicant's affidavit to the contrary as part of the permit application,[540] served on all tenants and posted in the building.

(d) Notice requirements.

Good faith is a generally required element in every notice. Like the most of the "just cause" eviction grounds, it is expressly mentioned in the statute's section 37.9(a)(10). Like the earlier-addressed ground for termination related to a condo-conversion, this ground is technically intensive and requires compliance with many prerequisite steps before the actual termination notice can be issued. Ability to identify and prevent a false or bad-faith application also seems to be the purpose of increasingly stricter regulations for the steps expected of an applicant-owner to comply with, required notices and declarations. The other side of this rule is that any noncompliance with any preceding requirement can be used to raise a presumption of bad faith.

It is recommended to include copies of the necessary obtained permits in order to avoid inviting an argument that permits were not obtained or not noticed to the tenant. It is further recommended to include a statement under Rule 12.19, notifying the recipients of an opportunity to return to the subject unit, should it become restored to its pre-notice housing use.

Other common elements applicable to this notice include most of the common elements covered in the "Commonly Required Notice Elements" section of this book apply, such as including the property description [¶ I(A)], parties [¶ I(B)], date and signature [¶ I(H)], information about the Rent Board [¶ I(I)], notice of an option to request initial inspection [¶ I(K)], notice of abandoning personal property [¶ I(J)], notice given in other languages [¶ I(M)], optionally also including the statement whether this notice supersedes other notices [¶ I(G)]. The notice has to include a statement of the lawful rent due [¶ III(U)], and landlord or agent's contact information [¶ III(V)]. A copy of the notice with its proof of service has to be filed with the Rent Board within 10 days from the service.

(e) Payments in connection with this termination ground.

Service of relocation payments is required in connection with the service of this type of termination notice. Unless the notice is issued when "landlord who seeks to demolish an unreinforced masonry building pursuant to Building Code Chapters 16B and 16C," relocation expenses are paid per S.F. Admin. Code, Sec. 37.9C. Otherwise—per S.F. Admin. Code, Sec. 37.9A(e).

If in any future iteration the Ordinance would require a payment in the amount higher than what is required under the "Ellis Act" ground (S.F. Admin. Code, Sec. 37.9A), such amendment runs a risk of being held unconstitutional and to be stricken down as it happened with Board's prior attempts in this direction.[364]

(f) Tenant's rights in connection with this ground for termination.

As covered above, tenants have a right to receive notice of the permit applications for the demolition, merger, or conversion of their rental unit. Tenants also have a right to appeal such permit applications to the S.F. Board of Appeals, and further have a right to appeal the already-issued permits within 15 days following issuance of the permit.[541]

Applicable to termination grounds under (a)(8)–(12) and including this one, the notice must inform a tenant of the restrictions in Ordinance Section 37.9(j),[542] the protection for households with child(ren) and so-called "educators." Landlord's request for tenant's information is made in writing.[543] This ground does not provide for an all-time protected status, only requiring that the termination notice has to expire within the San Francisco School District's summer break.

The tenant to whom those protections apply must advise the landlord in writing within 30 days if the tenant is claiming a "protected status" under Section 37.9(j). If a tenant fails to claim protected status within 30 days following service of the notice, the status is deemed waived.[544] Child- and "educator"-related protections are covered in Section ¶ III (Y), as they are available to several types of non-fault evictions.

(g) Section 8 application.

All the above-discussed requirements apply in the case of terminating a subsidized tenancy, in addition to any notice requirements by that subsidy program.[545]

An owner may terminate the subsidized tenancy for the "other good cause," which definition includes "A business or economic reason for termination of the tenancy (such as ... renovation of the unit).[546]"

The notice shall be at least 90 days long. It should include information not only about the portion tenants were paying, but also of what was paid by the program, and a copy of said notice should be filed with the Rent Board within 10 days after service of notice.[547] The tenants may not be obligated to pay more than their portion of rent during that 90-day period. The landlord, assuming the subject rental unit remains in existence and available for rent, will not be eligible to set an initial rent for five years following the date of termination, and the rate during those five years will remain the same as it was under the terminated subsidy program, plus the authorized increases under that subsidy program.[548]

A. Volkov. Eviction Notice In San Francisco.

This book came into existence with support of Melissa Volkov, and I am immeasurably thankful for her bearing with me through my late-night typing, while cutting corners on chores, family time, and changing diapers.

Special thanks go to my friends and colleagues, who helped me in uncounted ways to keep this book alive:

Sergey Avetikov
Roger Bernhardt
Dmitry Brodsky
Shawn Carberry
Vlad Chernoguz
Michael Chiu
Kung Yen Chiu
Michael Cramer
Oleg Fedorov
Phil Foster
Nate Freed
Valery Guralnik
Lee Heidhues
Peter Kelsch
Charles Kieser
Daniel Klausner
Tony Klein
Oxana Kozlov
Marina Krasner
Alla Lipovetsky
Michael Lipsky
Susanna Lorant
Jerry Marymont
Mychael Monroe

Alek Patek
George Polzer
Aleksandr Rabinovich
Rita Rabinovich
Ritu Raj
Charles Rosenberg
Patrick Ryan
Christine Tour-Sarkissian
Paul Tour-Sarkissian
Dmitry Semiannikov
Yuri Sokol
Drew Soto
Jerry Topolos
Wendy Topolos
Scott L Woodall
Kent Woods
Tanya & Lev Yurovsky
Paul Zinchik
Eugene Zinchik

NOTES

Footnotes:

1   www.seasonofsharing.org
2   *House v. Keiser* (1857) 8 Cal. 499, 501: "The statute "concerning forcible entry and unlawful detainer" is in derogation of the common law, and must be strictly construed."
3   "If a person breaks first into someone's dwelling, let him pay with 6 shillings." Æthelberht's code, ¶22, see also ¶¶ 28, 29 (602-603 A.D.).
4   "The Laws of King Alfred," §42. Fordham University translations of Old English Laws or Dooms. (http://legacy.fordham.edu/halsall/source/560-975dooms.asp).
5   Henry de Bracton mentions the laws of forcible entry and disseysine in his work (approximately dated 1235-1260). Per Bracton, there was already a 5-day rule in place and the possessor "must be ejected within five days, because the law of ancient time granted that the [evictor] should go one day to the East, the second day to the West, the third day to the South, and the fourth day to the North, to seek succour of his friends all the country round." Henry de Bracton, "De Legibus Et Consuetudini-bus Angliæ," book 4, edited by Sir Travers Twiss, (1880) London, Longman & Co., Vol. III, Introduction, p. xxxvii. ("Bracton") A possessor absent for a military of spiritual service was given a chance to delay eviction. (*Id.*) The case was set for trial within 15 days from tenant's "attachment to jurisdiction." (*Id.* at 161). The possession was obtained via writ, after judgment (*Id.*, at 15, 131, 139), and only after a complaint already made (35). Among the causes, unjust detention was already present (*Id.* at 15), as well as an entry by force (*Id.* at 23,25, 33). See also, Blackstone Commentaries, Book 3, Chapter X, Sec. II(1).
6   A possessor was given a chance to cure (Bracton, *supra,* 81) or quit (*Id.* at 77), or face a lawsuit if not cured or quitted, after a request had been made "by a man personally with a living voice" (*Id.* at 87, 89, 109).
7   Bracton, *supra,* 113, 615.
8   *Dickinson v. Maguire* (1858) 9 Cal. 46, 50, dates the development of forcible entry and forcible detainer law since the first Act of Parliament of 2 Ed. III. (Statute of Northampton, 1328); Blackstone puts the starting point at a more modern statute, 5 Ric. II. st.1. c.8. (The Forcible Entry Act of 1381), see Blackstone,

book IV, ch. 11, §8, Of Public Wrongs. In the very next wrong, of going armed, §9, Blackstone analogizes Statute of Northhampton with the laws of Solon (Greece, 6 B.C.).

[9] *Sullivan v. Cary* (1860) 17 Cal. 80, 85: "Our statute does not define the time or the necessity of such notice, but the common law is adopted, and includes the necessity."

[10] *Uridias v. Morrell* (1864) 25 Cal. 31, 35.

[11] William Taylor. California Life Illustrated, p. 19 (Carlton & Porter ed. 1858).

[12] See *e.g.* a case about eviction from the Mission Dolores property, *Warner v. Kelly* (1850) 1 Cal. 92.

[13] *Ladd v. Stevenson & Parker* (1850) 1 Cal. 18.

[14] The Residential Rent Stabilization and Arbitration Board, www.sfrb.org

[15] SF Admin. Code, Chapter 37.

[16] Evictions requiring no notice are permitted elsewhere in the state, but not applicable in San Francisco. S.F. Admin. Code, Section 37.9(c); *Bullard v. San Francisco Residential Rent Stabilization Bd.* (2003) 106 Cal.App.4th 488; *Gross v. Super. Ct.* (1985) 171 Cal.App.3d 265.

[17] *Knox v. Streatfield* (1978) 79 Cal.App.3d 565, 567.

[18] *Green v. Super. Ct. of San Francisco* (1974) 10 Cal.3d 616, 635.

[19] Hans Julius Wolff "Roman Law. A Historical Introduction." Oklahoma Press (1951), p.165.

[20] See *e.g.*, *Hollar v. Saline Products.* (1938) 25 Cal.App.2d 542, 544 [Where a tenant denies his landlord's title, the denial makes him a trespasser and he is not entitled to notice to quit before the commencement of an action by the landlord to recover possession of the premises].

[21] *Chan v. Antepenko* (1988) 203 Cal.App.3d Supp. 21; but see CC § 1946.5 for periodic lodging—notice is required.

[22] CC §§ 1940(b), 1865(c), 1866; *San Jose Parking, v. Super. Ct.* (2003) 110 Cal.App.4th 1321, 1329; *Bullock v. City & County of San Francisco* (1990) 221 Cal.App.3d 1072, 1097; *Sloan v. Court Hotel* (1945) 72 Cal.App.2d 308, 314; *Roberts v. Casey* (1939) 36 Cal.App.2d Supp. 767, 768; *Kibbee v. Blue Ridge Ins. Co.* (1999) 69 Cal.App.4th 53, 61-62.

[23] *Lawrence v. Ballou* (1869) 37 Cal. 518.

[24] CCP §§ 318–326.

25 *Karz v. Mecham* (1981) 120 CA3d Supp 1, 4; *Marquez-Luque v. Marquez* (1987) 192 Cal.App3d 1513, 1518–1519; unless converted to a periodic tenancy, see *Kong v. City of Hawaiian Gardens Redevelopment Agency* (2002) 101 Cal.App.4th 1317, 1331. But see, S.F. Admin. Code, Section 37.2(t), including the tenancy by sufferance in the definition of the "tenant."
26 CCP § 1160.
27 *Agar v. Winslow* (1899) 123 Cal. 587, 591; *Titus v. Canyon Lake Property Owners Ass'n* (2004) 118 Cal.App.4th 906, 914.
28 *Jacob v. Lorenz* (1893) 98 Cal. 332, 338.
29 *Lightner Mining Co. v. Lane* (1911) 161 Cal. 689, 695.
30 CC § 1951.3.
31 CCP §§ 1159, 1160, 1172, 1174. Sometimes a 5-day notice is required. CCP § 1160(2).
32 *City of Stockton v. Stockton Plaza Corp.* (1968) 261 Cal.App.2d 639, 656.
33 However, even for those exempt situations, consider that possession under some of those scenarios can still be argued as a "housing accommodation" covered by the eviction control if goes over 32 days. (S.F. Admin. Code, Sections 37.2(g) and (r)(1)).
34 The most current version and even some commentaries are published by the Rent Board online here: http://sfrb.org/ordinance-regulations. The official online publisher of the current version of the San Francisco municipal codes, including the Administrative Code and its Chapter 37, is the American Legal Publishing Corp. (www.amlegal.com).
35 S.F. Admin. Code, Section 37.2(2), first sentence, mentions "all residential dwelling units."
36 S.F. Admin. Code, Section 37.9(a)(4)(B): "residential occupancy of a unit not authorized for residential occupancy by the City."
37 http://sfrb.org/fact-sheet-1-general-information
38 http://www.sfrb.org/index.aspx?page=1036
39 Section 8 evictions falling under CCP § 1161, still require a notice in compliance with that statute. *Gersten Cos. v. Deloney* (1989) 212 Cal.App.3d 1119, 1128.
40 24 CFR §§ 982.310, 983.257; 42 USC §§ 1437d, 1437f(d)(1)(B).
41 CC § 1954.535; *Wasatch Property Mgmt. v. Degrate* (2005) 35 Cal.4th 1111, 1123.

---

42   Gov. C §65863.10(b) and (c), generally applicable for multi-unit buildings, subsidized under several recognized programs, including project-based Section 8.

43   24 CFR 982.310(e)(ii)(2)(ii).

44   Such as a disclosure of right to grievances hearing under 24 CFR 966.50, see also Gov. C §65863.10 for its own required information in the notice.

45   24 CFR § 982.1, 42 USC 1437f.

46   24 CFR § 982.1(a)(3); the term "voucher" is defined in 24 CFR § 982.4(b).

47   24 CFR § 982.1(a)(3).

48   S.F. Admin. Code, Sec. 37.2(r)(4)(A).

49   S.F. Admin. Code, Sec. 37.2(r)(4)(B).

50   S.F. Admin. Code, Sec. 37.3(f)(3).

51   S.F. Admin. Code, Section 37.1, File No. 188-79, Ordinance No. 276-79.

52   S.F. Admin. Code, Section 37.9, first sentence.

53   S.F. Admin Code, Section 56, enacted in 1988 [Ordinance 372-88].

54   S.F. Admin Code, Section 37.9D(a) and (b).

55   S.F. Admin Code, Section 37.3(d)(1)(A); see also, the definition of a "rental unit" in Section 37.2(r).

56   S.F. Admin Code, Section 37.3(d)(2)(A) (i)–(iii).

57   Termination notices under CC §§ 827, 1946, are expressly mentioned in Section 37.3(d)(1)(A), while the referred-to Costa Hawkins Act includes CC § 1946.1 [See, CC § 1954.52(a)(3)(B)(i)].

58   S.F. Admin. Code, Section 37.3(d)(1)(C) excludes a property "which contains serious health, safety, fire or building code violations, excluding those caused by disasters for which a citation has been issued by the appropriate governmental agency and which has remained unabated for six months or longer preceding the vacancy."

59   http://www.sfrb.org/index.aspx?page=1037   and http://www.sfrb.org/index.aspx?page=1038

60   S.F. Admin. Code, Section 37.2(l); Residential Rehabilitation Loan Program, Chapter 32, San Francisco Administrative Code.

61   S.F. Admin. Code, Section 37.9D.

62   S.F. Admin. Code, Section 37.9(b); S.F. Rent Ordinance, Topic No. 210; see also, Topic No. 019. CC § 1946.5 mentions "a lodger" in singular form.

63 *Chun v. Del Cid* (2019) 34 Cal.App.5th 806, 819, reh'g denied (May 25, 2019).

64 S.F. Rent Ordinance, Rules and Regulations, Rule 6.15C(1).

65 *Chan v. Antepenko* (1988) 203 Cal.App.3d Supp. 21, 25: "those who actually reside in the rooms and pay their rent in the form of in-lieu wages are licensees and have no protection under the Rent Ordinance"; but see *Spinks v. Equity Residential Briarwood Apartments* (2009) 171 Cal.App.4th 1004, 1041.

66 S.F. Rent Ordinance, Topic No. 019; S.F. Admin. Code, Section 37.2(r)(4)(D).

67 Ordinance No. 30-15, as amended by Ordinances Nos. 162-16, 95-17 and 162-17. For summary of terms, see DBI Information Sheet G-23, available online at: http://sfdbi.org/sites/default/files/IS%20G-23%20Word.docx

68 Pub.L. No. 111-22, div. A, tit. VII, §§ 702–704 (May 20, 2009) 123 Stat. 1660, as amended in 2010, Pub.L. No. 111-203, tit. XIV, § 1484.

69 *Nativi v. Deutsche Bank National Trust Co.*, 223 Cal.App.4th 261, 267 (2014).

70 S.F. Admin. Code, Section 37.9D(b).

71 S.F. Admin. Code, Section 37.9D(e) and CC § 1962.

72 S.F. Admin. Code, Section 37.9D(e)(iii).

73 *Gross v. Super. Ct.* (1985) 171 Cal.App.3d 265, 274.

74 An eviction under Section 37.9(a)(7) still requires a written notice to already vacated tenant, with whom that relationship had been previously established. See Section 37.9(c).

75 *Santa Monica Rent Control Bd. v. Bluvshtein* (1991) 230 Cal.App.3d 308, 316.

76 *Santa Monica Rent Control Bd, supra.*

77 *Goodman v. Community Sav. & Loan Asso.* (1966) 246 Cal.App.2d 13.

78 *Plaza Freeway v. First Mt. Bank* (2000) 81 Cal.App.4th 616, 626; but see, *Robert T. Miner, M.D., Inc. v. Tustin Ave. Investors* (2004) 116 Cal.App.4th 264, 272 [when the estoppel certificate contains an ambiguous reference to a term].

79 *Tanzola v. De Rita* (Cal. 1955) 45 Cal.2d 1, 9; *Boehle v. Benson* (1957) 150 Cal.App.2d 696, 701.

80 CC §§ 1946, 1946.1; CCP § 1161(2)(3), and (5). See how CC § 1946.1(a) addresses the absence of a written notice.

81 The San Francisco Residential Rent Stabilization and Arbitration Ordinance, Chapter 37 of the San Francisco Administrative Code.

82 S.F. Admin. Code, Sections 37.2(r), 37.3(d), and 37.9.

83 Sir Edward Coke. Institutes of the Laws of England, Part I, Vol.2, [212.a.] Sect. 342.

84 S.F. Rent Ordinance, Rules and Regulations, Rules 6.15A, 6.15B.

85 S.F. Health Code, Article 19M.

86 Judicial Form UD-100 of Unlawful Detainer complaint, for optional use, p.2, ¶¶6e, 6f.

87 CACI 4302 through 4309.

88 CACI 4301.

89 Judicial Form UD-100 of Unlawful Detainer complaint, for optional use, p.2, ¶7e.

90 Judicial Form UD-100 of Unlawful Detainer complaint, for optional use, p.2, ¶8d.

91 *Hinman v. Wagnon* (1959) 172 Cal.App.2d 24, 29.

92 *Colyear v. Tobriner* (1936) 7 Cal.2d 735, 742.

93 *King v. Connolly* (1872) 44 Cal. 236, 238-239.

94 S.F. Rent Board, "Topic No. 210: Evictions of Roommates and Subtenants," available at http://www.sfrb.org/index.aspx?page=971; S.F. Rent Board, "Topic No. 019: Partial Exemption for Certain Single-Family Homes and Condominiums Under Costa-Hawkins," available at http://www.sfrb.org/index.aspx?page=1038

95 *University of Southern California v. Weiss* (1962) 208 Cal.App.2d 759. For a detailed discussion and distinctions as to various types of occupants, see Rutter Group, Cal. Prac. Guide Landlord-Tenant (through Sept. 2017 update), Ch. 7-C, ¶¶ 7:179–7:182, 7:184–7:185.1.

96 CC §§ 1431, 1659.

97 http://sfrb.org/part-6-rent-increase-justifications

98 D. Wasserman "The Unhappy Handshake" (SFAA, 2015); S. Fester "Roommate Roulette" (SFAA; 2012); C. F. Dowling "One is the Loveliest Number" (SFAA; 2009); A. J. Wiegel & C. E. Fried "Section 6.14 and the Costa-Hawkins Act" (SFAA; 2004).

99 "Moving-in the Subtenants: Sensitive Time Limits under the Rules 6.15A and 6.15B" (ponfo.blogspot.com; Aug. 2013).

100 CCP §§ 415.46, 715.020(d), 1174.25, 1174.3; Judicial Forms CP-10, CP-10.5.

[101] CCP § 1161(2), eviction for non-payment of rent.

[102] CC § 1962. See also, S.F. Admin. Code, Section 37.9(k).

[103] CCP § 1161a(a)(3), *Dr. Leevil, LLC v. Westlake Health Care Center* (2018) 6 Cal.5th 474, 482.
See also, S.F. Admin. Code, Sec. 37.9D(e).

[104] *Barela v. Super. Ct.* (1981) 30 Cal.3d 244.

[105] *Lester v. Isaac* (1944) 63 Cal.App.2d Supp. 851;
DeZerega v. Meggs (2000) 83 Cal.App.4th 28.

[106] *Lester v. Beer* (1946) 74 Cal.App.2d Supp. 984.

[107] S.F. Admin. Code, Section 37.9(c), first sentence.

[108] CC §§ 1946, 1946.1.

[109] S.F. Admin. Code, Section 37.9 is applicable only to "housing units" as defined in Section 37.2(r).

[110] S.F. Admin. Code, Section 37.3(d).

[111] S.F. Admin. Code, Section 37.9(a); *Danekas v. S.F. Rent Board*, 95 Cal.App.4th 638, 698–702 (2001) [Municipalities have legislative authority to adopt rules and regulations regarding evictions]; *Birkenfeld v. City of Berkeley* (1976) 17 Cal.3d 129, 147–150 [substantive limitations are Ok], but see *Id.* at 150–153 [procedural limitations interfering with statelaw and summary process of eviction are not Ok].

[112] S.F. Admin. Code, Section 37.9 is applicable only to "rental units" as defined in Section 37.2(r), with an exception under 37.2(r)(7), if conditions of 37.3(d) apply.

[113] CCP §§ 1161, 1161a, 1161b, 1161c; CC §§ 789, 1946, 1946.1, 1954.535; Govt C § 7060.4; S.F. Admin. Code, Sections 37.9, 37.9A, 37.9B, 37.9C.

[114] Judicial Form UD-100 of Unlawful Detainer complaint, for optional use, p.2, ¶7b.

[115] *Ray v. Armstrong* (1854) 4 Cal. 208; *Lamanna v. Vognar* (1993) 17 Cal.App.4th Supp. 4; *Kruger v. Reyes* (2014) 232 Cal.App.4th Supp. 10 [also covers prematurely served notice itself].

[116] *Bauer v. Neuzil* (Cal.App. Dep't Super. Ct., 1944) 66 Cal.App.2d Supp 1020; *Levitz Furniture Co. v. Wingtip Communications* (2001) 86 Cal.App.4th 1035, fn.1 [five days were given under a 3-day notice]. Effective September 2019, notices under CCP § 1161(2) and (3) exclude from its total time "Saturdays and Sundays and other judicial holidays."

---

117 *Telegraph Ave. Corp. v. Raentsch* (1928) 205 Cal. 93, 99; CC § 1946 [by agreement to shorten the period by to no less than 7 days]; *Fifth & Broadway Partnership v. Kimny* (1980) 102 Cal.App.3d 195, 200; *Kruger v. Reyes* (2014) 232 Cal.App.4th Supp. 10; *Hsieh v. Pederson* (2018) 23 Cal.App.5th Supp. 1, 7.

118 See also, CC § 1942.5(c), S.F. Admin. Code, Section 37.9(d).

119 CCP § 1161(2) says so directly; CC § 1946 implies by proposing language re: personal property and offering to "contact your former landlord." See also, CC § 1962.

120 S.F. Admin. Code, Sections 37.9(a)(8), 37.9(a)(9), 37.9(a)(10), 37.9(a)(11), 37.9(a)(12), 37.9(a)(14), 37.9(a)(15); See also, *See also, Bumgarner v. Orton* (1944) 63 Cal.App.2d Supp. 841, 843; *Lester v.* Isaac (1944) 63 Cal.App.2d Supp. 851, 853 [decided on based on war-era ordinance, requiring statement of good faith in the notice]; *Drouet v. Super. Ct.* (2003) 31 Cal.4th 583.

121 CC § 1942.5(e).

122 S.F. Admin. Code, Sections 37.9(c), 37.9(d), 37.9(e); *Rental Housing Assn. of Northern Alameda County v. City of Oakland* (2009) 171 Cal.App.4th 741, 759.

123 *Lindenberg v. MacDonald* (1950) 34 Cal.2d 678.

124 CC § 1942.5; S.F. Admin. Code, Sections 37.9(d).

125 See CC § 1942.5(a), no such requirement for the lessee under CC § 1942(c).

126 CC § 1947.7.

127 *Horton-Howard v. Payton* (1919) 44 Cal.App. 108, 115. See also, *Turney v. Collins* (1941) 48 Cal.App.2d 381, 392, and fn. 11.

128 See, *e.g., Asell v. Rodrigues* (1973) 32 Cal.App.3d 817, 821.

129 Rutter Group, Cal. Prac. Guide Landlord-Tenant (through Oct. 2018 update), Ch. 7-C, ¶ 7:110.2 ["Cautious landlords may deem it more prudent to serve separate three-day notices in the event of simultaneous breaches of the rent and other lease covenants. This approach clearly establishes the right to proceed on each notice as a separate cause of action and thus avoids the possibility that a court might view the failure to prove all alleged breaches as rendering a combined three-day notice defective"].

130 *Rental Housing Assn. of Northern Alameda County v. City of Oakland* (2009) 171 Cal.App.4th 741, 759.

131 *Castle Park No. 5 v. Katherine* (1979) 91 Cal.App.3d Supp. 6.

[132] As it is often necessary, when the recovery of possession is coupled with the need to recover pre-termination rent, not recoverable unless a separate notice under CCP § 1161(2) is served. *Saberi v. Bakhtiari* (1985) 169 Cal.App.3d 509, 512-517.

[133] "We conclude that section 12.20 permits eviction based upon a unilaterally imposed term of tenancy that is authorized by the Rent Ordinance or required by federal, state or local law ..." Unpublished decision, *Hayes v. Kardosh*, No. A142573, 2017 WL 1382566, at *12 (Cal. Ct. App. Apr. 18, 2017), as modified on denial of reh'g (May 16, 2017), review denied (July 19, 2017).

[134] *Cavanaugh v. High* (1960) 182 Cal.App.2d 714, 721.

[135] *Earl Orchard Co. v. Fava* (1902) 138 Cal. 76, 79.

[136] *Zumwalt v. Hargrave* (1945) 71 Cal.App.2d 415, 419-420.

[137] *McCormick v. Marcy* (1913) 165 Cal. 386, 392: "One tenant in common may recover possession of the whole estate against all persons except his cotenants, and his recovery inures to the benefit of his cotenants."

[138] *Axis Petroleum Co. v. Taylor* (1941) 42 Cal.App.2d 389, 396; see also, *Bank of America Nat. Trust & Savings Ass'n v. Button* (1937) 23 Cal.App.2d 651; *Wayland v. Latham* (1928) 89 Cal.App. 55, 66–67, citing Civil Code §§ 821, 1111, holding that an assignee or an agent can maintain an eviction action.

[139] S.F. Admin. Code, Section 37.9(a)(8)(iii).

[140] In case the notice was signed by the same attorney who will be later conducting the trial, it will be procedurally impracticable to provide that attorney as a witness.

[141] Cal. Evid. Code § 1413. See also, Cal. Evid. Code §§ 1411, 1412 [a subscribing witness is no longer required to authenticate a document, but remains as one of the options to do so].

[142] Cal. Landlord-Tenant Litigation, Ch. 1, ¶4.09 (Mathew Bender).

[143] S.F. Admin. Code, Section 37.9(c), fourth sentence.

[144] C §§ 1946, 1946.1, 1950.5, 1983, 1984, 1985, 1987, 1988, and 1990. [2012 Cal AB 2521, 2012 Cal ALS 560].

[145] CA Landlord-Tenant Litigation, Ch. 1, ¶4.23 (Mathew Bender); CEB California Eviction Defense Manual (06/2014), Ch.6, ¶6.13.

[146] *Korens v. R. W. Zukin Corp.* (1989) 212 Cal.App.3d 1054, reh'g denied.

[147] The State Act includes self-collectors in the definition of the "debt collector" Civ. Code, § 1788.2(c), while those collectors are

148 *Jerman v. Carlisle et al.* (2010) 559 U.S. 573.

149 http://sfrb.org/forms-center#sec6

150 CC § 2924.8.

151 CC § 3485.

152 CC § 3486.

153 CC § 1632(b) and (d).

154 *Long Beach Brethren Manor, Inc. v. Leverett* (2015) 239 Cal.App.4th Supp. 24 [a material breach under Section 8 lease still required a 30-day notice, not a 3-day allowed under CCP 1161(3)].

155 S.F. Admin. Code, Section 37.9(h). See also, Section 37.9(g) and corresponding definitions of applicable tenancies under Section 37.2(r)(4)(A) and (B).

156 *Naylor v. Super. Ct.* (Cal. Super. Ct., 2015) 236 Cal.App.4th Supp. 1, 2, an appeal from the case *Hirsch v. Naylor*, CUD-14-650718.

157 *Housing Authority of the City & County of S.F. v. Blissett* (CUD-02-601424), S.F. Super. Ct., May 06, 2002.

158 CC § 1946, CC § 1946.1(f); *Liebovich v. Shahrokhkhany* (1997) 56 Cal.App.4th 511, 517, footnote 2.

159 *Highland Plastics, Inc. v. Enders* (1980) 109 Cal.App.3d Supp. 1, 7; *Losornio v. Motta* (1998) 67 Cal.App.4th 110, as modified.

160 Rutter Group, Cal. Prac. Guide Landlord-Tenant Ch. 7-C, Bases for Terminating Tenancy, ¶7:220.3: "It is unclear whether the CCP § 1013 mail service extension might apply in that situation." See also, *Highland Plastics, Inc. v. Enders* (1980) 109 Cal.App.3d Supp. 1, 9-10, discussion on whether the notice requires to act, and the dissent opinion of J. Saeta, *Id.* at 14. Further, a non-fault termination notice in San Francisco does require a tenant to act in several ways, including by making timely requests within the period of the notice.

161 CCP § 415.45.

162 CCP § 1162(a)(3).

163 *University of Southern California v. Weiss* (1962) 208 Cal.App.2d 759, 769 citing *Gentry v. Citron* (1918) 36 Cal.App. 288.

164 *Briggs v. Electronic Memories & Magnetics Corp.* (1975) 53 Cal.App.3d 900, 905: "Merely providing subtenant with a copy of the notice directed to and served on tenant is not sufficient,

Above: generally excluded from the Federal Act definitions, see 15 USCS § 1692a.

since it merely demands that tenant pay rent or quit, not that subtenant do so."

[165] *Cowell v. Linforth* (1909) 10 Cal.App. 3, 5; *Zucco v. Farullo* (1918) 37 Cal.App. 562, 568.

[166] CACI 4303, 4305, 4307, 4309; *Bank of New York Mellon v. Preciado* (2013) 224 Cal.App.4th Supp. 1, 7: "A notice is valid and enforceable only if the lessor has strictly complied with these statutorily mandated requirements for service."

[167] *Palm Property Investments v. Yadegar* (2011) 194 Cal.App.4th 1419, 1426.

[168] *Palm Property Investments v. Yadegar, supra,* at 1427, citing Friedman et al., Cal. Practice Guide: Landlord-Tenant (The Rutter Group 2010) ¶¶ 9:204.1 to 9:204.2, p. 9-54 (rev. # 1, 2009).

[169] The Residential Rent Stabilization and Arbitration Board of the City and County of San Francisco, 25 Van Ness Avenue, Suite No. 320, San Francisco, CA 94102. Telephone: (415) 252-4600.

[170] S.F. Admin. Code, Section 37.9(c), fifth sentence.

[171] S.F. Admin. Code, Section 37.9B(c).

[172] S.F. Rent Ordinance, Rules and Regulations, Rule 12.17.

[173] 24 CFR 982.310(e)(ii)(2)(ii).

[174] The Chapter 8 of the US Housing Act of 1937 (42 USC § 1437f), not the "Section 8" part of the UK Housing Act of 1988, defining eviction grounds used in England and Wales.

[175] The San Francisco Housing Authority, 1815 Egbert Ave, San Francisco, CA 94124. Telephone: (415) 715-3280.

[176] CCP § 12, 12a, 12b.

[177] *Reclamation Dist. No. 535 v. Hamilton* (1896) 112 Cal. 603, 612. [service of a proposed statement is not invalid or void because made on Sunday or a legal holiday].

[178] *Kruger v. Reyes* (2014) 232 Cal.App.4th Supp. 10.

[179] *Bullard v. San Francisco Residential Rent Stabilization Bd.* (2003) 106 Cal.App.4th 488, 492.

[180] *Highland Plastics, Inc. v. Enders* (1980) 109 Cal.App.3d Supp. 1, 7; *Losornio v. Motta* (1998) 67 Cal.App.4th 110, 115.

[181] *Walters v. Meyers* (1990) 226 Cal.App.3d Supp. 15, 20.

[182] *Davidson v. Quinn* (1982) 138 Cal.App.3d Supp. 9, 14.

[183] S.F. Admin. Code, Section 37.9(a).

[184] S.F. Admin. Code, Section 37.9(a)(1)(A).

185 S.F. Admin. Code, Section 37.9(c) [provided that it is the 3-day notice].

186 *Hinman v. Wagnon* (1959) 172 Cal.App.2d 24, 29.

187 CCP § 1161(2).

188 CCP § 1161(2); *Kruger v. Reyes* (2014) 232 Cal.App.4th Supp. 10.

189 CCP § 1161(2) as amended effective September 1, 2019.

190 *Fifth & Broadway Partnership v. Kimny* (1980) 102 Cal.App.3d 195, 200; *Kruger v. Reyes* (2014) 232 Cal.App.4th Supp. 10; *Hsieh v. Pederson* (2018) 23 Cal.App.5th Supp. 1, 7.

191 See, *e.g.*, *Hindin v. Caine* (1951) 104 Cal.App.2d 238, 241.

192 CC § 1947; *Rosenbaum Estate Co. v. Robert Dollar Co.* (1916) 31 Cal. App. 576, 577.

193 *See, Lee v. Silverman* (2004) CUD-04-612066, Feb 25, 2005, judgment on summary motion for the tenant in "habitually late" case, even though grace period was expressly segregated in the lease as not adding time to the due date (decision based on established prior conduct between the parties).

194 10 Cal. Real Est. § 34:70 (4th ed.) Miller and Starr, California Real Estate § 34:70, citing *Baypoint Mortgage Corp. v. Crest Premium Real Estate etc. Trust* (1985) 168 Cal. App. 3d 818, 831.

195 *Kruger v. Reyes* (2014) 232 Cal.App.4th Supp. 10, 17–18 [distinguishing the payment performance under CC § 1500], see also, *Mau v. Hollywood Commercial Bldgs., Inc.* (1961) 194 Cal.App.2d 459, 470. *Bawa v. Terhune* (2019) 33 Cal.App.5th Supp. 1, 9.

196 *Boyd v. Carter* (2014) 227 Cal.App.4th Supp. 1, 10.

197 *Levitz Furniture Co. v. Wingtip Communications* (2001) 86 Cal.App.4th 1035, 1043.

198 *Levitz Furniture Co. v. Wingtip Communications* (2001) 86 Cal.App.4th 1035, 1038, citing *Ernst Enterprises v. Sun Valley Gasoline* (1983) 139 Cal.App.3d 355, 359.

199 "[P]ast-due rent was necessarily an overstatement of defendant's rental obligation, which could only be properly calculated as zero." *N. 7th St. Assocs. v. Constante* (2016) 7 Cal. App. 5th Supp. 1, 5.

200 *Johnson v. Sanches* (1942) 56 Cal.App.2d 115; *Dertiman v. Almey* (1949) 92 Cal.App.2d 724; *Werner v. Sargeant* (1953) 121 Cal.App.2d 833.

201 *Nourafchan v. Miner* (1985) 169 Cal.App.3d 746 [excess of $5.86].

202 *Gruzen v. Henry* (1978) 84 Cal.App.3d 515, 519 [excess of $18].

203 *Bawa v. Terhune* (2019) 33 Cal.App.5th Supp. 1, 9.

204 *Ambrose RP, Inc. v. Mimie Cove* (CUD-12-642567), S.F. Super. Ct., Oct. 19, 2012.

205 *Chase v. Peters* (1918) 37 Cal.App. 358, 361. See also for further discussion, *Harris v. Bissell* (1921) 54 Cal.App. 307, 313–314.

206 *Del Monte Properties and Investments, Inc. v. Dolan* (2018) 26 Cal.App.5th Supp. 20.

207 *Cavanaugh v. High* (1960) 182 Cal.App.2d 714.

208 CC §§ 1962(f), 1476. *Sleep EZ v. Mateo* (2017) 13 Cal.App.5th Supp. 1, 10 [Sec. 1476 "provided defendants' obligation to pay rent was extinguished by performance in the manner plaintiff specified, even though plaintiff did "not receive the benefit of such performance""].

209 *DLI Properties LLC v. Hill* (2018) 29 Cal.App.5th Supp. 1, 9 [the landlord escaped in that case only because the court held it was a new owner with a new lease, rather than a subsequent owner stepping into an existing lease].

210 S.F. Admin. Code, Sections 37.9(k), 37.9D(e).

211 *Foster v. Williams* (2014) 229 Cal.App.4th Supp. 9, 17.

212 CCP § 1174(a).

213 *Neuhaus v. Norgard* (1934) 140 Cal.App. 735, 739–740.

214 24 CFR 247.4(c); *Gersten Cos. v. Deloney* (1989) 212 Cal.App.3d 1119.

215 See, *e.g.*, for the one of the voucher programs (CFR, Title 24, Section 982), the obligation to pay rent and landlord's right to evict are spread over three statutes: CFR 982.515(c), 24 CFR 982.551(e), and 24 CFR 982.310(a)(1) ["failure to pay rent" is deemed a "serious violation"]; for a corresponding provision in the Project subsidy program (24 CFR 247), see 24 CFR 247.3(a)(1) and (c)(4) ["Non-payment of rent" is one of the instances of "material incompliance"].

216 CCP § 1161.5.

217 Sir Edward Coke. Institutes of the Laws of England, Part I, Vol.2, [211.b.] Sect. 341. (L.3, C.5. Sect. 341 [211.b.])

218 *Kern Sunset Oil Co. v. Good Roads Oil Co.* (1931) 214 Cal. 435, 440.

219 *Gould v. Corinthian Colleges, Inc.* (2011) 192 Cal.App.4th 1176, 1179.

220 *Karbelnig v. Brothwell* (1966) 244 Cal.App.2d 333.

221 *Edc Assocs. v. Gutierrez* (1984) 153 Cal.App.3d 167, 170.

[222] *Little v. Sanchez* (1985) 166 Cal.App.3d 501.

[223] *Chen v. Kraft* (2016) 243 Cal.App.4th Supp. 13, 22, citing CC § 1958.

[224] *Salton Community Services Dist. v. Southard* (1967) 256 Cal.App.2d 526.

[225] *Sabi v. Sterling* (2010) 183 Cal.App.4th 916, 935: "[a] simpler way of stating the point is that [Section 8] assistance payments to the landlord are not included in the tenant's income."

[226] California Gov. Code, Section 12955 (p)(1).

[227] *Giebeler v. M&B Assocs.* (9th Cir. 2003) 343 F.3d 1143.

[228] *N. 7th St. Assocs. v. Constante* (2016) 7 Cal.App.5th Supp. 1, 5.

[229] A. Volkov "In Leasing an "In-Law" Apartment Don't Be "In Pari Delicto" - Beware of an Exception for Legal Enforcement of Illegal Contracts" (2013), citing S.F. Rent Board Topic No. 253, *Corrie v. Soloway* (2013) 216 Cal.App.4th 436; *Carter v. Cohen* (2010) 188 Cal.App.4th 1038; *Salazar v. Maradeaga* (1992) 10 Cal.App.4th Supp. 1.

[230] *Wang v. Xu Hua Jie* (CUD-07-623371), S.F. Super. Ct., Oct. 24, 2007.

[231] CC § 1946.1(b).

[232] See S.F. Admin. Code, Section 37.9(k)(1)(A) re: mandatory disclosure "that tenants cannot be evicted or asked to move solely because a property is being sold or solely because a new owner has purchased that property."

[233] CC § 791; *Hennessy v. Gleason* (1947) 81 Cal.App.2d 616, 619 (month to month); *La Cava v. Breedlove* (1946) 77 Cal.App.2d 129 (fixed term expired)

[234] CC § 790; *Nicolaysen v. Pacific Home* (1944) 65 Cal.App.2d 769, 773.

[235] *Kingston v. Colburn* (1956) 139 Cal.App.2d 623, 625: "Necessarily therefore the notice of January 11 was insufficient and not in compliance with the statute so as to terminate the tenancy on January 10, but that is not to say it would not have been effective as of February 10."

[236] S.F. Admin. Code, Section 37.9(a); see also, *DeZerega v. Meggs* (2000) 83 Cal.App.4th 28, decided under the Berkeley Rent Ordinance.

[237] S.F. Rent Board "Fact Sheet 4 – Eviction Issues," "Overview of "Just Cause" Eviction Issues."

238 CC §§ 1943, 1944, 1945, 1946, 1947.
239 CC § 1962(a),(b).
240 CC § 1962(f).
241 CC § 1962(c), last sentence.
242 *Four Seas Inv. Corp. v. International Hotel Tenants' Assn.* (1978) 81 Cal.App.3d 604, 611–612.
243 CC § 1962(c) and (f).
244 CC § 1950.5(f)(1).
245 *Saberi v. Bakhtiari* (1985) 169 Cal.App.3d 509, 515.
246 *E.g.*, in a form complaint UD-100, page 3, ¶17(e), strike "forfeiture" and replace it with "termination."
247 CC §§ 790, 791, 793.
248 *Drybread v. Chipain Chiropractic Corp.* (2007) 151 Cal.App.4th 1063, 1075; *Mitchell Land & Improvement Co. v. Ristorante Ferrantelli* (2007) 158 Cal.App.4th 479, 491. But see, *North 7th St. Assocs. v. Constante* (2016) 7 Cal. App. 5th Supp. 1, 4–5, citing *Kwok v. Bergren* (1982) 130 Cal.App.3d 596, 599–600, for a proposition that evictions under CCP § 1161 are not based on contract, but rather on the statute.
249 *Salton Community Services Dist. v. Southard* (1967) 256 Cal.App.2d 526, 531.
250 *Gersten Cos. v. Deloney* (1989) 212 Cal.App.3d 1119, 1129.
251 *Four Seas Inv. Corp. v. International Hotel Tenants' Assn.* (1978) 81 Cal.App.3d 604, 611–612.
252 S.F. Admin. Code, Section 37.9(a)(1)(C).
253 *People v. Sanchez* (2003) 105 Cal.App.4th 1240, 1244.
254 The payment must be either cashed or returned within 30 days. S.F. Admin. Code, Section 37.10B(a)(11) and (12).
255 CC § 1719.
256 Cal. Pen. Code § 476a.
257 S.F. *Admin.* Code, Section 37.9(a)(2)(D), as added effective Nov. 9, 2015.
258 *Hinman v. Wagnon* (1959) 172 Cal.App.2d 24, 27; *Delta Imps. v. Mun. Court* (1983) 146 Cal.App.3d 1033, 1036. Same exclusion from the 3-day count of "Saturdays and Sundays and other judicial holidays," under CCP § 1161(3) as under 1161(2), effective September 1, 2019.
259 S.F. Admin. Code, Section 37.9(a)(2), last sentence, as it reads in the version effective Nov. 9, 2015.

[260] *Webb v. Jones* (1927) 88 Cal.App. 20, 34: "The failure of defendants to fulfill the other covenants not to alter the premises without consent and to keep the premises furnished are sufficient to sustain the judgment terminating the lease with no right of reinstatement."

[261] As defined in S.F. Admin. Code, Section 41.4(p).

[262] S.F. Admin. Code, Section 37.9(a)(2)(A).

[263] S.F. Admin. Code, Section 37.9(a)(2)(B)(i) and (ii).

[264] S.F. Admin. Code, Section 37.9(c)(2).

[265] S.F. Admin. Code, Section 37.9(a)(2);
see also, *Boston LLC v. Juarez* (2016) 245 Cal.App.4th 75, 82-83.

[266] Rutter Group, Cal. Practice Guide, Landlord-Tenant (2014), ¶7:130, citing *NIVO 1 LLC v. Antunez* (2013) 217 Cal.App.4th Supp. 1, 5, for the discussion of a trivial breach, and *Hignell v. Gebala* (1949) 90 Cal.App.2d 61, 66, for the bar of this defense in intentional breach.

[267] *Cal-American Income Property Fund Iv v. Ho* (1984) 161 Cal.App.3d 583, 585.

[268] A. Volkov. Ordinance Alters Landlord-Tenant Relationship. The Recorder (March 6, 2012).

[269] S.F. Rent Board "Fact Sheet 4 – Eviction Issues," "Overview of 'Just Cause' Eviction Issues"; *Foster v. Britton* (2015) 242 Cal. App. 4th 920.

[270] 24 CFR 982.310(a)(1).

[271] *Feder v. Wreden Packing & Provision Co.* (1928) 89 Cal.App. 665, 671.

[272] *Swords to Plowshares v. Smith* (N.D. Cal. 2002) 294 F.Supp.2d 1067, 1073, analyzing also the requirement for specificity of the notice under 24 CFR 274.

[273] *Swords v. Kemp* (N.D. Cal. 2005) 2005 U.S. Dist. LEXIS 41284, 3, 2005 WL 3882063.

[274] *Samantha Lee Seto Property Mngmt v. Bet Ching Gee et al.* (CUD-16-657307), S.F. Super. Ct., Order on demurrer, January 13, 2017.

[275] *Mendoza v. Frenchman Hill Apts. Ltd. P'ship* (E.D. Wash. 2005) 2005 U.S. Dist. LEXIS 47373, 7, 2005 WL 6581642; *In re Di Giorgio* (9th Cir. 1998) 134 F.3d 971, 975.

[276] *Horneff v. City and County of San Francisco* (2003) 110 Cal.App.4th 814, 818.

[277] *McCord v. Oakland Quicksilver Mining Co.* (1883) 64 Cal. 134, 140.

[278] *Dieterich Internat. Truck Sales, Inc. v. J. S. & J. Services* (1992) 3 Cal.App.4th 1601, 1610.

[279] *Smith v. Cap Concrete, Inc.* (1982) 133 Cal.App.3d 769, 777-778 [leaving concrete debris on property was found a permanent and market *value*-reducing act, even though the concrete could be removed and value thus restored].

[280] *Mohilef v. Janovici* (1996) 51 Cal.App.4th 267, 302.

[281] *Wilms v. Hand*, (1951) 101 Cal.App.2d 811.

[282] Cal. Penal Code §§ 631, 632, 632.5-632.7. But see, *People v. Guzman* (2017) 11 Cal.App.5th 184, 191 [re: Sec. 632(d) in criminal proceedings, held it unconstitutional as to recording a confidential communication without the consent of all parties].

[283] SF Penal Code, Section 36.

[284] *Salton Community Services Dist. v. Southard* (1967) 256 Cal.App.2d 526, 529: "Where a covenant in a lease has been breached and the breach cannot be cured, a demand for performance is not a condition precedent to an unlawful detainer action."

[285] Rent Ordinance's Topic No. 258. See also, California Fair Employment and Housing Act, Gov-t Code § 12900, *et seq.*; Federal Fair Housing Act, 42 U.S.C. 3601 *et seq.*

[286] 24 CFR 982.310(d)(ii).

[287] *Cadigan Arbor Park v. Vohra* (Cal.App. Dep't Super. Ct., 2006) 2006 Cal. App. LEXIS 2159, 2: "The notice was thus inadequate as it did not put defendant on notice of the acts he needed to defend against."

[288] SF Admin. Code, Chapter 41A, Sec. 41A.4, Definition of "Residential Unit."

[289] *Chen v. Kraft*, 243 Cal.App.4th Supp., *supra*, at 21.

[290] *Kaufman v. Goldman* (2011) 195 Cal.App.4th 734, 745.

[291] *Bedford v Eastern Bldg. & Loan Assoc.* (1901) 181 US 227; *Home Bldg. & Loan Asso. v Blaisdell* (1934) 290 US 398.

[292] *Chen v. Kraft*, 243 Cal.App.4th Supp., *supra*, at 22, citing CC § 1598.

[293] *Cohen v. Ratinoff* (1983) 147 Cal.App.3d 321, 329.

[294] 24 CFR 982.310(c)(1) and 24 CFR 982.310(c)(2)(i)(C).

[295] *Birkenfeld v. City of Berkeley* (1976) 17 Cal.3d 129, 148.

[296] *Parkmerced Co. v. San Francisco Rent Stabilization & Arbitration Bd.* (1989) 215 Cal.App.3d 490, 496. Applicable also to holdover

cases following foreclosure sales and evictions under CCP § 1161a. *Gross v. Super. Ct.* (1985) 171 Cal.App.3d 265, 276.

[297] S.F. Admin. Code, Section 37.2(t); *Chan v. Antepenko* (1988) 203 Cal.App.3d Supp. 21, 23-24.

[298] *Chaney v. Schneider* (1949) 92 Cal.App.2d 88, 92.

[299] *Glenn v. Bacon* (1927) 86 Cal.App. 58, 72: "if there be any ambiguity or uncertainty—that ambiguity or uncertainty must be resolved in favor of the lessee, the lessor being the scrivener. (Sec. 1654, Civ. Code.)"

[300] CC § 1945.

[301] CC § 1945.

[302] *Ellis v. Columbine Creamery Co.* (1927) 83 Cal.App. 48, 55.

[303] *Ryland v. Appelbaum,* (1924) 70 Cal.App. 268.

[304] CCP § 1161(1).

[305] The "effective date of this ordinance" is generally understood as referring to the date of June 13, 1979. [S.F. Admin. Code, Section 37.1] However, the effective date of applying the exemptions of 37.2 is August 24, 1980, [Section 37.9] which would only be material for the leases commenced before that date. "Substantial Rehabilitation" is defined in Section 37.2(s).

[306] CC §§ 1933(1), 793; CCP § 1161(1).

[307] Such statutes are CC §§ 1946, 1946.1, 827; and the requirements mentioning these are stated in SF Admin. Code, Section 37.3(d)(1)(A) and CC § 1954.52(a)(3)(B)(i).

[308] CC § 827(a).

[309] CC § 827(b)(2).

[310] CC § 827(b)(3).

[311] The highest recorded increase of 7% was allowed in the period from April 1, 1982, through February 29, 1984. Since March 1, 1993, and through today, the rate never went over 2.9%.

[312] 24 CFR 982.310(d)(1)(i).

[313] CC § 1954.535; S.F. Admin. Code, Section 37.3(d)(3)(A).

[314] CC § 1954(e), (d)(1).

[315] CC § 1954(d)(1)–(3).

[316] http://www.sfrb.org/index.aspx?page=975

[317] *Dwyer v. Carroll* (1890) 86 Cal. 298, 304–305 [If there is no provision to the contrary in the lease, the landlord may reenter the premises to effect necessary repairs. The landlord may not,

however, reenter to make major alterations without the tenant's permission].

[318] CC § 1954(c).

[319] CC § 1940.2(4).

[320] *Dromy v. Lukovsky* (2013) 219 Cal.App.4th 278, 286.

[321] CCP § 1160(2); see also, *Wong v. Enrique Nova et al.*, (CUD-15-651054), S.F. Super. Ct., Mar. 30, 2015, where eviction was sought based on a 5-day notice under CCP §§ 1159, 1160.

[322] *Pacific States Auxiliary Corp. v. Farris* (1931) 118 Cal.App. 522.

[323] *Frazier v. Hanlon* (1855) 5 Cal. 156;
Merrill v. Forbes (1863) 23 Cal. 379.

[324] *Rimmer v. Blasingame* (1892) 94 Cal. 139.

[325] *Roberts v. Casey* (1939) 36 Cal.App.2d Supp. 767, 774.

[326] *Marquez-Luque v. Marquez* (1987) 192 Cal.App.3d 1513, 1518–1519.

[327] *Ryland v. Appelbaum* (1924) 70 Cal.App. 268, 270 [no notice even when the lease contained a holdover clause].

[328] S.F. Admin. Code, Section 37.9(c). This includes a "tenant at sufferance," but does not include a licensee, lodger, or a former employee. *Chan v. Antepenko* (1988) 203 Cal.App.3d Supp. 21; but see *Spinks v. Equity Residential Briarwood Apartments* (2009) 171 Cal.App.4th 1004, 1041.

[329] S.F. Admin. Code, Section 37.2(t).

[330] *Uridias v. Morrell* (1864) 25 Cal. 31, 35; *Hauxhurst v. Lobree* (1869) 38 Cal. 563, 563, citing Blackstone Commentaries, Book 2 [Chap. IX, Sec. III].

[331] *Danger Panda, LLC v. Launiu* (2017) 10 Cal.App. 5th 502, 515 [not every lawful occupant is also a tenant].

[332] *Danekas v. San Francisco Residential Rent Stabilization & Arbitration Bd.* (2001) 95 Cal.App.4th 638.

[333] Civil Code § 1954.53(d)(2) and (d)(4) provide for a landlord to establish new rent rate when all original tenants vacate and deem acceptance of rent not a waiver of landlord's rights, yet the very next subsection (e) explains that these provisions (addressing the rights to increase rent) shall not be "construed to affect any authority of a public entity that may otherwise exist to regulate or monitor the grounds for eviction."

[334] S.F. Rent Ordinance, Rules and Regulations, Rule 6.14(b)–(d).

335 *Danekas v. San Francisco Residential Rent Stabilization & Arbitration Bd.* (2001) 95 Cal.App.4th 638, 648.

336 Under *Danekas, supra,* at 648, at least four factors are used in conjunctive.

337 6.15A(c); 6.15B(b); 6.15D(b); 6.15E(b).

338 *Mosser Cos. v. San Francisco Rent Stabilization & Arbitration Bd.* (2015) 233 Cal.App.4th 505, 507; review denied (Apr. 29, 2015); *T & A Drolapas & Sons v. San Francisco Rent Stabilization & Arbitration Bd.* (2015) 238 Cal.App.4th 646.

339 *Danger Panda, LLC v. Launiu* (2017) 10 Cal.App. 5th 502, 522.

340 *200 Arguello Assocs., LLC v. Dyas* (Cal. Ct. App. May 12, 2017) No. A145533, 2017 WL 1967748, at *14.

341 *Glenn v. Bacon* (1927) 86 Cal.App. 58, 72, citing Civ. Code § 1654.

342 *ASP Properties Group, L.P. v. Fard, Inc.* (2005) 133 Cal.App.4th 1257, 1272.

343 *Chan v. Antepenko* (1988) 203 Cal.App.3d Supp. 21, 26.

344 *Karz v. Mecham* (1981) 120 Cal.App.3d Supp. 1, 4.

345 See also, *Cobb v. San Francisco Residential Rent Stabilization & Arbitration Bd.* (Cal.App. 1st Dist., 2002) 98 Cal.App. 4th 345.

346 24 CFR 982.551(h).

347 24 CFR 982.309 (c)(2).

348 24 CFR 982.312 (a) and (b).

349 CC § 1947.10 [Owner or relative move-in]; CC § 1940.6 [demolition of the unit]; CC § 1954.535 [extending notice time for government subsidized rentals]; Gov-t Code § 7060.4 [Ellis Act notice].

350 Form UD-100, page 2, ¶7(d).

351 *Castle Park No. 5 v. Katherine* (1979) 91 Cal.App.3d Supp. 6; *Saberi v. Bakhtiari* (1985) 169 Cal.App.3d 509, 515.

352 *E.g.,* in a form complaint UD-100, page 3, ¶17(e), strike "forfeiture" and replace it with "termination."

353 *Palmer v. Zeis* (1944) 65 Cal.App.2d Supp. 859, 862; accord, *Hennessy v. Gleason* (1947) 81 Cal.App.2d 616, 619.

354 *Castle Park No. 5 v. Katherine* (1979) 91 Cal.App.3d Supp. 6.

355 *Chacon v. Litke* (2010) 181 Cal.App.4th 1234, 1248–1249.

356 S.F. Admin. Code, Section 37.9(a)(2).

357 See *e.g.,* CC § 1954.535 (90 days for government-subsidized tenancies); S.F. Admin. Code, Section 37.9(j)(1) extending time for OMI evictions until the next school-year break for households with children; S.F. Admin. Code, Section 37.9A(f)(4) providing for

extension of time to a year in Ellis Act evictions for disabled and elderly.

[358] CC § 1946, first sentence, as amended for extending time to 60 days by CC § 1946.1. See also, *Wheeler v. Bainbridge* (1948) 84 Cal.App.2d Supp. 849 (notice there was given on October 13 to terminate on November 13).

[359] CC § 1946, 2d sentence, as interpreted by *Miller & Desatnik Mgmt. Co. v. Bullock* (1990) 221 Cal.App.3d Supp. 13, 18.

[360] S.F. Admin. Code, Section 37.3(d)(3)(A).

[361] S.F. Admin. Code, Section 37.9C(c) and (d).

[362] S.F. Admin. Code, Section 37.9(i)(4).

[363] S.F. Admin. Code, Section 37.9C(e)(2).

[364] *Levin v. City & County of San Francisco* (N.D. Cal. Oct. 21, 2014) 71 F.Supp.3d 1072, 1086, appeal denied as moot 680 Fed.Appx. 610, judgment upheld on remand, 257 F.Supp.3d 1092 (May 30, 2017); *Jacoby v. City & County of San Francisco* (CGC-14-540709, Judgment entered on March 19, 2015), S.F. Super. Ct, affirmed, *Coyne v. City and County of San Francisco* (2017) 9 Cal.App.5th 1215, review denied (June 28, 2017).
Both cases favored striking down certain relocation assistance payments as too high. A general requirement of providing assistance when tenancy is terminated is within municipal powers. *Pieri v. City and County of San Francisco* (2006) 137 Cal.App.4th 886 [decided under the Ellis Act].

[365] S.F. Admin. Code, Section 37.9(i)(4) & 37.9(j)(3), see also, S.F. Admin. Code, Section 37.9A(f)(4) & 37.9C(e)(2).

[366] S.F. Admin. Code, Section 37.9C(a)(1).

[367] S.F. Admin. Code, Section 37.9C(d), first sentence. Amount may need be adjusted for the increase, if the rates were recalculated during those 180 days.

[368] S.F. Admin. Code, Section 37.9C(d), last sentence.

[369] S.F. Admin. Code, Section 37.9(A)(e).

[370] S.F. Admin. Code, Section 37.9(a)(10), last sentence.

[371] A landlord may still elect to provide for relocation payments. Park Merced did so in 2015, agreeing to pay in accordance with Section 37.9C, to those relocating tenants who declined to take a replacement unit.

[372] S.F. Admin. Code, Section 37.9C(b).

[373] S.F. Admin. Code, Section 37.9C(e)(2).

[374] Entitlement to payments requires 12 month of more, while requirements under the statute of frauds and alike are for over one year: CC §§ 1091, 1624(d), and CCP § 1971.

[375] *Pieri v. City and County of San Francisco* (Cal.App. 1st Dist., 2006) 137 Cal.App.4th 886, reh'g denied, *Pieri v. City & County of San Francisco* (2006, Cal.App. 1st Dist) 2006 Cal App LEXIS 375, review denied, *Pieri v. City & County of San Francisco* (2006, Cal.) 2006 Cal LEXIS 7613.

[376] *Levin v. City & County of San Francisco* (N.D. Cal. Oct. 21, 2014) 71 F. Supp. 3d 1072, 1086; *Jacoby v. City & County of San Francisco* (CGC-14-540709), S.F. Super. Ct., Judgment entered on March 19, 2015, invalidating Ordinance 54-14. See also, *Coyne* (CPF-15-514382), S.F. Super. Ct., Order from October 2, 2015, invalidating Ordinance 68-15.

[377] Publication 529, available at: http://www.sfrb.org/Modules/ShowDocument.aspx?documentid=1928

[378] San Francisco Subdivision Code, Section 1396(e) [the ban is not absolute, there are exemptions under (e)(B)–(D)]. See also, S.F. Subdiv. Code, Sections 1396.2(a)&(e), 1396.4(b)(10).

[379] S.F. Admin. Code, Section 37.3(d)(1)(A) and 37.3(f)(1).

[380] S.F. Admin. Code, Section 37.9A(a), 37.9B(a), 37.9B(b).

[381] CC § 1947.15(k).

[382] S.F. Admin. Code, Section 37.9(c), first sentence; Rule 12.17 (as amended 9-11-2018).

[383] S.F. Admin. Code, Section 37.3(f)(3).

[384] *Title Ins. & Trust Co. v. Amalgamated Oil Co.* (1923) 63 Cal.App. 29, 34; *Fahrenbaker v. E. Clemens Horst Co.* (1930) 209 Cal. 7, 9; *Hindin v. Caine* (1951) 104 Cal.App.2d 238, 241.

[385] S.F. Admin. Code, Section 37.3; see there, 37.3(a)(10) for a different treatment in limiting rents in government-subsidized tenancies.

[386] SFHA fair market rent / payment standard, most recently updated in 2016. http://www.sfha.org/SFHA_Payment_Standards_1-1-2016.pdf

[387] CC § 827, CC § 1954.535; Fact Sheet 7 (for S.F. Rent Ordinance). For Section 8 treatment, see, *e.g.*, 24 CFR 982.1(a)(2), 24 CFR 982.308(g)(4), 24 CFR 503(a)–(b), 24 CFR 982.519(b)(6), 24 CFR 982.520.

[388] S.F. Admin. Code, Section 37.9C(a)(2).

[389] Ordinance 55-16, approved April 22, 2016.

[390] *SFAA v. CCSF* (2018) 20 Cal.App.5th 510, review denied (Apr. 25, 2018), reversing (S.F. Super. Ct., 2016) CPF-16-515087.

[391] S.F. Admin. Code, Section 37.9(j)(1). For more definitions, see 37.9(j)(4).
For determining the length of the San Francisco School Year, visit the website of the San Francisco Unified School District, at: http://www.sfusd.edu/en/news/calendars/academic-calendar.html

[392] Proposed as S.F. Admin. Code, Section 37.9(j)(4).

[393] S.F. Admin. Code, Section 37.9(i)(4), 37.9(j)(3).

[394] S.F. Admin. Code, Section 37.9C(e)(2): "[the payment] shall be paid within fifteen (15) calendar days of the landlord's receipt of written notice from the Eligible Tenant of entitlement to the relocation payment along with supporting evidence." Similar rule is for an Ellis Act eviction, Section 37.9A(e)(3)(C), although it is silent on "supporting evidence."

[395] S.F. Admin. Code, Section 37.9(j)(2).

[396] S.F. Admin. Code, Section 37.9(j)(1).

[397] See *e.g.*, S.F. Admin. Code, Section 37.9(a)(10), (a)(15).

[398] Residential mergers, unless subject to Conditional Use, shall be prohibited. S.F. Planning Code, Sec. 317(f);
see also Sec. 101.1(b)(3) for the statement of preservation of housing as a reason.

[399] S.F. Planning Code, Sec. 317(g)(2), last par. Compare, *S.F.A.A. v. CCSF* (2016) 3 Cal. App.5th 463, invalidating Sec. 317(e)(4), which was proposing a 10-year ban on mergers after Ellis Act evictions. Similar effect in *SPOSFI v. CCSF* (2018) 22 Cal.App.5th 77, attacking 5 / 10-year waiting period ordinance on renovations of units following non-fault evictions under Sec. 181(c).

[400] http://www.sf-planning.org/index.aspx?page=2816

[401] S.F. Rent Ordinance, Topic No. 019.

[402] S.F. Planning Code, Section 317(b)(13).

[403] S.F. Planning Code, Section 317(d), (e), and (f).

[404] *Cwynar v. City* (2001) 90 Cal.App.4th 637. [a regulation precluding or limiting landlords' right to reclaim their real property is reviewed under elevated scrutiny standard of whether the "ordinance substantially advanced a legitimate government interest"], see also, CC § 1947.10(a).

[405] S.F. Admin. Code, Section 37.9(a)(8)(i).

[406] See, *e.g.*, Cal. Evid. Code § 175, CCP § 680.280, Cal. Bus & Prof Code § 2032.

407 *Investors Equity Life Holding Co. v. Schmidt* (2015) 233 Cal.App.4th 1363, 1380.

408 Case of Sutton's Hospital (1612) 5 Rep. 303; 10 Rep. 32b.

409 *Carne v. Worthington* (2016) 246 Cal.App.4th 548, 564; *Reilly v. City and County of San Francisco* (2006) 142 Cal.App.4th 480, 488-490.

410 "[T]he "trust is not an entity separate from the trustees," and "the trustee, rather than the trust, is the real party in interest in litigation involving trust property."" *Jenson v. Allison-Williams Co.* (S.D.Cal. 1999), CASE NO: 98-CV-2229 TW (JFS)) 1999 U.S. Dist. LEXIS 22170, at *30, citing *Moeller v. Super. Ct.* (1997) 16 Cal.4th 1124, 1132 n.3. See also, *McKoin v. Rosefelt* (1944) 66 Cal.App.2d 757, 768; *Allan v. Guaranty Oil Co.* (1917) 176 Cal. 421. Similarly, it is also possible for a trustee to sue for a wrongful eviction. *Igauye v. Howard* (1952) 114 Cal.App.2d 122.

411 S.F. Admin. Code, Section 37.9(a)(8)(vi).

412 Cal Bus & Prof Code § 11212(x)–(z).

413 *Azar v. Rodriguez* (2017) CUD-15-653804, appel. div. decision Apr. 26, 2017.

414 S.F. Admin. Code, Section 37.9(a)(8)(iv).

415 *Bullard v. San Francisco Residential Rent Stabilization Bd.* (2003) 106 Cal.App.4th 488, 493, applying Costa-Hawkins Act, CC § 1954.53. See also, *Palmer/Sixth Street Properties, L.P. v. City of Los Angeles* (2009) 175 Cal.App.4th 1396, 1408-1409.

416 Either by not satisfying the parameters of protection for age or disability under Section 37.9(i)(1), or waiving the right to claim such protection, under Section 37.9(i)(4).

417 *Bakanauskas v. Urdan* (1988) 206 Cal.App.3d 621, 627.

418 S.F. Admin. Code, Section 37.9B(c)(6); S.F. Rent Ordinance, Rules and Regulations, Rule 12.14(b)(6).

419 S.F. Admin. Code, Section 37.9C(c); S.F. Rent Ordinance, Rules and Regulations, Rule 12.14(b)(7).

420 Form 579 (multi-lingual), or the top of the 2d page of Form 577 (English version).

421 *Naylor v. Super. Ct.* (2015) 236 Cal. App. 4th Supp. 1, 8–9, 186 Cal.Rptr.3d 791, 796: "[t]he requirement ... to give notice of "the tenant's or lessee's right[] to reoccupancy" does not say "all possible nuances that might arise under possible future factual scenarios..." ... the Termination Notice here did not unreasonably

or unfairly address that subject by referral to the relevant text of the rent ordinance."

[422] See *e.g.*, *Jin Ping Chen Mak v. Juan Carlos Ramirez* (CUD-16-655918), S.F. Super. Ct., Order from Sept. 22, 2016; *Irizarry v. Ruiz* (CUD-16-657049), S.F. Super. Ct., Order from Jan. 25, 2017.

[423] *Garber v. Levit* (2006) 141 Cal. App. 4th Supp. 1 [Proposition G's 25% *ownership* requirement for owners acquiring an interest in the property prevailed over the Bierman Amendment's 50% ownership requirement.]

[424] S.F. Admin. Code, Section 37.9(a)(8)(iii).

[425] S.F. Bus. & Tax Reg. Code, Article 12-C, see *e.g.*, Sections 1102 (Imposition of the tax) and 1105 (Exemptions).

[426] *Tom v. City and County of San Francisco* (2004) 120 Cal.App.4th 674.

[427] S.F. Admin. Code, Section 37.9B(a), first sentence; Section 37.3(f).

[428] S.F. Admin. Code, Section 37.9B(c)(5); S.F. Rent Ordinance, Rules and Regulations, Rule 12.14(f)(3)(iii). "The offer to re-rent must be filed at the Rent Board within 15 days of the offer." Topic No. 203; see also S.F. Admin. Code, Section 37.9B(b)(2).

[429] S.F. Admin. Code, Section 37.9(a)(8)(vi).

[430] S.F. Rent Ordinance, Rules and Regulations, Rule 12.14(b)(1)–(11).

[431] Form 1007.

[432] Form 958; see also, S.F. Admin. Code, Section 37.9(a)(8)(v); Rule 12.17 (as amended 9-11-2018).

[433] S.F. Admin. Code, Section 37.9C(e)(2).

[434] Also see, S.F. Admin. Code, Section 37.9(a)(8)(vii).

[435] S.F. Rent Ordinance, Rules and Regulations, Rule 12.14(f)(1); Form 546A.

[436] S.F. Rent Ordinance, Rules and Regulations, Rule 12.14(f)(2) and (4); Form 546B.

[437] S.F. Rent Ordinance, Rules and Regulations, Rule 12.14(f)(3); Form 546C.

[438] S.F. Rent Board "Fact Sheet 4 – Eviction Issues," "Overview of "Just Cause" Eviction Issues." [due for an update, current version is dated April 2010]

[439] S.F. Admin. Code, Sections 37.9(i)(4) and (j)(3), first sentence in both, requires "a written request" or "a notice of termination of tenancy."

[440] S.F. Admin. Code, Section 37.9(i)(4).

[441] S.F. Admin. Code, Section 37.9(j)(3).

[442] S.F. Admin. Code, Section 37.9(a)(i)(1).

[443] S.F. Admin. Code, Section 37.9(i)(4) and (j)(3).

[444] "Rental Information Questionnaire" form, published by the S.F. Assoc. of Realtors®. See also, S.F. Admin. Code, Section 37.9(k)(1)(E); *Robert T. Miner, M.D., Inc. v. Tustin Ave. Investors* (2004) 116 Cal.App.4th 264 [terms of the lease and estoppel are analyzed together, with ambiguity enforced against the landlord].

[445] *DeLaura v. Beckett* (2006) 137 Cal.App.4th 542, 546-547.

[446] S.F. Admin. Code, Sections 37.9(f), 37.9(j).

[447] *Jankowski Lee & Associates v. Cisneros*, 91 F.3d 891, 895 (7th Cir. 1996), cited together with other relevant authority in *Smith v. Powdrill*, 2013 U.S. Dist. LEXIS 154485, 15-16, 2013 WL 5786586 (C.D. Cal. Oct. 28, 2013).

[448] *200 Arguello Assocs., LLC v. Dyas*, No. A145533, 2017 WL 1967748, at *4 (Cal. Ct. App. May 12, 2017), S. F. trial case No. CGC–15–544426.

[449] S.F. Admin. Code, Section 37.9(i)(1)(A).

[450] S.F. Admin. Code, Sections 37.9(i)(1)(B) and 37.9(i)(1)(B)(i).

[451] S.F. Admin. Code, Sections 37.9(i)(1)(B) and 37.9(i)(1)(B)(ii).

[452] S.F. Admin. Code, Section 37.9(i)(2).

[453] *Bakanauskas v. Urdan* (1988) 206 Cal.App.3d 621, 629–630 [Regular grant deed, as the one we have, does not violate subdivision laws. Without naming specifically, takers of title are presumed tenants in common. TIC agreement for exclusive use is proper and enforced in OMI eviction], citing CC § 686, *Conde v. Dreisam Gold Mining Co.* (1906) 3 Cal. App. 583. "Due to the high cost of acquiring residential real property in certain California cities in the past decade, many home buyers acquire multi-unit buildings as TIC, and then the TIC make agreements among themselves, to give each owner an exclusive right of occupancy (ERO) in a particular dwelling unit within the overall TIC property." *Tom v. City and County of San Francisco* (2004) 120 Cal.App.4th 674, 677. [SF Ordinance proposing to prohibit ERO was found unconstitutional]. "[T]he entire purpose of a TIC is to allow home ownership to those who cannot afford single-family homes." *Id.* at 681. City's potentially laudable goal in providing more rental housing is not enough a reason to block TIC-EROs. *Id.* at 687.

[454] S.F. Admin. Code, Sections 37.9(a)(8)(iv) and (v); S.F. Rent Ordinance, Rules and Regulations, Rules 12.14(a)(8) and 12.14(e).

[455] CC § 1947.10(a).

[456] S.F. Admin. Code, Section 37.9(a)(8)(iv), last sentence.

[457] S.F. Admin. Code, Section 37.9(a)(8)(v), last sentence.

[458] S.F. Rent Ordinance, Rules and Regulations, Rule 12.14(e)(6)–(8).

[459] *Bullard v. San Francisco Residential Rent Stabilization Bd.* (2003) 106 Cal.App.4th 488, 492, decided under a prior version of OMI regulations.

[460] *Geraghty v. Shalizi* (2017) 8 Cal. App. 5th 593, 598.

[461] Compare, S.F. Admin. Code, Section 37.9(a)(8)(i) and 37.9(a)(8)(ii).

[462] S.F. Admin. Code, Sections 37.9(a)(8)(v)(2) and (3).

[463] *Rental Housing Assn. of Northern Alameda County v. City of Oakland* (2009) 171 Cal.App.4th 741, 757.

[464] S.F. Admin. Code, Section 37.9(a)(8)(vii); S.F. Rent Ordinance, Rules and Regulations, Rule 12.14(f)(1)–(4).

[465] S.F. Admin. Code, Section 37.9(a)(8)(vii), last 2 sentences; S.F. Rent Ordinance, Rules and Regulations, Rule 12.14(f)(6).

[466] S.F. Admin. Code, Section 37.9(a)(8)(vii); S.F. Rent Ordinance, Rules and Regulations, Rule 12.14(f)(5).

[467] *Sylve v. Riley* (1993) 15 Cal.App.4th 23, decided under an older version of the ordinance.

[468] S.F. Admin. Code, Section 37.3(f), 37.3(f)(1).

[469] See, *e.g.*, S.F. Admin. Code, Sections 37.9B(c) and 37.9C(c).

[470] S.F. Admin. Code, Section 37.9C(e)(1), as indexed.

[471] S.F. Admin. Code, Section 37.9(a)(8)(iv).

[472] S.F. Admin. Code, Section 37.9(h).

[473] 24 CFR 982.310(a)(3) and 24 CFR 982.310(d)(1)(iii).

[474] CC § 1954.535 (part of the Costa-Hawkins Act); S.F. Admin. Code, Section 37.3(d)(3)(A)–(C). S.F. Admin. Code, Section 37.3(f) and (f)(1).

[475] S.F. Admin. Code, Section 37.3(f)(3).

[476] S.F. Admin. Code, Section 37.9(a)(8)(ii).

[477] Oakland Mun. Code, Section 8.22.360 A.9.

[478] Without saying more, I may only relay that an order sustaining tenant's demurrer on this ground was issued in S. F. Trial Court in 2017.

[479] On the current (2013) moratorium, see 11-20-17 order on motion to dismiss (Doc #25) in 3:17-cv-03638, *Pakdel v. CCSF*, 2017 WL 6403074 (currently on appeal, No. 17-17504): "[t]he City's objectives in imposing the lifetime lease requirement are expressly articulated in the Ordinance and pass rational basis review." On the earlier (1982) moratorium, see, *Leavenworth Properties v. City* (1987) 189 Cal.App.3d 986 [City's moratorium on condominium conversion did not deprive apartment building owner of equal protection of the laws because the ordinance was rationally related to the legitimate state interest of maintaining affordable rental housing.] See also, *Hock Investment Co. v. City and County of San Francisco* (1989) 215 Cal.App.3d 438, 448.

[480] *San Francisco Apt. Ass'n v. City & County of San Francisco*, CPF-14-513452, 2014 Cal. Super. LEXIS 4795, *37-38 (Cal. Super. Ct., Nov. 25, 2014), upheld on appeal, *SFAA v. CCSF* (2016) 3 Cal.App.5th 463.

[481] *McMullan v. Santa Monica Rent Control Bd.* (1985) 168 Cal.App.3d 960.

[482] *Griffin Dev. Co. v. City of Oxnard* (1985) 39 Cal.3d 256, 263 [The scrutiny test for an ordinance affecting owner's property rights in condo conversion is whether "the ordinance is reasonably related to a legitimate governmental purpose." *Id.* at 265]; *Bownds v. City of Glendale* (1980) 113 Cal.App.3d 875 [Municipality had authority to establish master development plan fitting local conditions and approve condominium conversion projects without strictly complying with advisory development guidelines established by state housing agency]; *Hazon-Iny Development v. City of Santa Monica* (1982) 128 Cal.App.3d 1; *Soderling v. City of Santa Monica* (1983) 142 Cal.App.3d 501 [City could enact ordinances imposing requirements for health and safety, including installation of smoke detectors, before approving projects converting structures to condominiums]; *California Bldg. Industry Assn. v. City of San Jose* (2015) 61 Cal.4th 435 [a requirement that a the developer sell 15 percent of its units at an affordable housing price]. But see, *Krater v. City of Los Angeles* (1982) 130 Cal.App.3d 839, holding that scarcity of replacement housing alone is not sufficient to deny a condo-conversion application.

[483] *Tom v. City and County of San Francisco* (2004) 120 Cal.App.4th 674.

A. Volkov. Eviction Notice In San Francisco.

---

484 *Thierman v. Public Works Dep't of San Francisco*, 2004 Cal. Super. LEXIS 651, *2, 2006 WL 204991 (not published appeal from CPF-04-504550), citing *Griffin Development Co. v. City of Oxnard*, 39 Cal.3d, *supra*, at 264-65; *Leavenworth Properties v. City and County of San Francisco* (1987) 189 Cal.App.3d 986, 991.

485 *Hock Investment Co. v. City and County of San Francisco* (1989) 215 Cal.App.3d 438 [new municipal regulations could not apply retroactively to an already issued permit for condo conversion]. See also on the issue of timing, *City of W. Hollywood v. Beverly Towers* (1991) 52 Cal.3d 1184; *City of W. Hollywood v. 1112 Investment Co.* (2003) 105 Cal.App.4th 1134; *Blue Chip Properties v. Permanent Rent Control Bd.* (1985) 170 Cal.App.3d 648.

486 S.F. Admin. Code, Section 37.9(a)(9).

487 Mainly, applicable sections for the tenancy-related regulations are in set in Article 9 of the Subd. Code, Sec. 1380, *et seq.*

488 The sale of the unit to a bona fide purchaser is a significant element. It exempts the unit from the rent control provisions under the Costa Hawkins Act. CC § 1954.52(a)(3)(B)(ii). "Condominium units are included in the third exemption, because they are alienable separate from the title to any other dwelling unit." *Burien, LLC v. Wiley* (2014) 230 Cal.App.4th 1039, 1045. This 2001 amendment to Costa Hawkins Act was "necessary to close a loophole in law that allows landlords to avoid local rent control laws." *City of West Hollywood v. 1112 Investment Co.* (2003) 105 Cal.App.4th 1134, 1143, as modified on denial of reh'g (Feb. 25, 2003).

489 S.F. Subdivision Code, Section 1383.

490 S.F. Subdivision Code, Sections 1387, 1988.

491 Gov-t Code, Sections 66427.1, 66452.17–66452.20.

492 S.F. Subdivision Code, Sections 1381(a)(3) and (a)(4)(D).

493 S.F. Subdivision Code, Section 1386.

494 S.F. Subdivision Code, Section 1396.2(a), only on non-fault grounds (a)(8), (a)(10), (a)(11), and (a)13). Note that actual evictions count, not notices for evictions [Sec. 1396.2(a)(1)], but a notice may be deemed an eviction if the notice was not withdrawn before expiration or a tenant does not remain in occupancy for 120 days after the notice expired. [Sec. 1396.2(e)]. See also, Sec. 1396(e)(2).

495 S.F. Subdivision Code, Section 1396.2(f).

496 S.F. Subdivision Code, Sections 1396.2(b), 1396(e)(2).

---

497 S.F. Subdivision Code, Sections 1396.2(f), 1359, 1396.1(g)(1) and (g)(3).

498 S.F. Subdivision Code, Section 1396.2(f).

499 S.F. Subdivision Code, Section 1396(e)(4); S.F. Admin. Code, Section 37.9E(e)(4);

500 *San Francisco Apartment Association v. CCSF* (9th Cir. 2018) 881 F.3d 1169, 1175.

501 *Small Property Owners of San Francisco Institute v. CCSF* (2018) 22 Cal.App.5th 77, review denied (June 20, 2018), attacking S.F. Planning Code, Section 181.

502 *San Francisco Apartment Association v. CCSF* (2016) 3 Cal.App.5th 463, attacking S.F. Planning Code, Section 317.

503 As explained in *Reidy v. CCSF* (2004) 123 Cal.App.4th 580, 591, as modified on denial of reh'g (Nov. 23, 2004).

504 *Griffin Development Co. v. City of Oxnard* (1985) 39 Cal.3d 256, 262.

505 S.F. Subdivision Code, Section 1396(e)(3)(A).

506 Tenant's right of first refusal is also codified on state level, Gov-t Code Sections 66427.1, 66452.20, see also, *Greenberg v. Super. Ct.* (1982) 131 Cal.App.3d 441.

507 S.F. Subdivision Code, Sections 1381(a)(6)(A) and 1381(a)(6)(B).

508 S.F. Subdivision Code, Section 1381(a)(6)(C): "Notice of the proposed conversion must be given to all persons or parties who lease or reside in any units which are proposed for conversion subsequent to approval of the application for conversion"—it is unclear if it is for subsequently proposed units or for subsequently leasing tenants in already proposed units.

509 S.F. Subdivision Code, Section 1387.

510 S.F. Subdivision Code, Section 1395.

511 S.F. Admin. Code, Section 37.9C(a)(1).

512 S.F. Subdivision Code, Section 1391(b), referring to CC § 1946. For government assisted tenancies' 90 days, see Civ. Code, Sec. 1954.535, 24 CFR 982.310(a)(3) and (d)(1)(iii) or (iv).

513 S.F. Subdivision Code, Sections 1391(a) [120 days], 1391(b) [termination notice to be given "upon expiration" of the requirements stated in Sec. 1391(a)].

514 *Pongputmong v. City of Santa Monica* (1993) 15 Cal.App.4th 99, 106.

515 S.F. Subdivision Code, Sections 1391(a), 1392, 1393.

516 S.F. Subdivision Code, Sections 1392(b), 1393(b).

517 S.F. Subdivision Code, Section 1392(b).

518 *Burien, LLC v. Wiley* (2014) 230 Cal.App.4th 1039, 1049.

519 *Golden State Ventures, LLC v. City of Oakland Rent Board* (Cal. Ct. App., Jan. 25, 2018, No. A151421) 2018 WL 549174, appeal from Alameda Court case No. RG16834166.

520 S.F. Subdivision Code, Section 1391(c).

521 *Pakdel v. CCSF* (N.D. Cal., Nov. 20, 2017, No. 17-CV-03638-RS) 2017 WL 6403074, at *5, currently on appeal.

522 S.F. Rent Board "Fact Sheet 4 – Eviction Issues," "Overview of "Just Cause" Eviction Issues." [might be updated, current version is from 2010]

523 S.F. Admin. Code, Sections 37.9(j)(3), first sentence, requires "a written request" or "a notice of termination of tenancy."

524 S.F. Admin. Code, Section 37.9(j)(3).

525 *Lincoln Place Tenants Ass'n v. City of Los Angeles* (2007) 155 Cal.App.4th 425, 451, as modified on denial of reh'g (Oct. 10, 2007).

526 *Valnes v. Santa Monica Rent Control Bd.* (1990) 221 Cal.App.3d 1116.

527 *Daro v. Super. Ct.* (2007) 151 Cal.App.4th 1079, 1100, as modified on denial of reh'g (July 3, 2007).

528 S.F. Admin. Code, Section 37.9(h).

529 24 CFR 982.310(a)(3) and 24 CFR 982.310(d)(1)(iv).

530 CC § 1954.535 (part of the Costa-Hawkins Act); S.F. Admin. Code, Section 37.3(d)(3)(A)–(C); S.F. Admin. Code, Section 37.3(f) and (f)(1).

531 S.F. Admin. Code, Section 37.3(f)(3).

532 See discussion in a change-of-use decision in *Bullock v. City and County of San Francisco* (1990) 221 Cal.App.3d 1072 [landlord intended to convert residential hotels to tourist use, analyzed under the Ellis Act].

533 *San Francisco Apartment Assn. v. City and County of San Francisco* (2016) 3 Cal.App.5th 463, 477.

534 *Small Property Owners of San Francisco Institute v. City and County of San Francisco* (2018) 22 Cal.App.5th 77, 88, review denied (June 20, 2018).

535 *Reidy v. City and County of San Francisco* (2004) 123 Cal.App.4th 580, 593, as modified on denial of reh'g (Nov. 23, 2004), analyzing

2000 and 2004 versions of the Ellis Act and whether a city ordinance could prevent a residential property owner to exist rental market.

[536] See, *First Presbyterian Church of Berkeley v. City of Berkeley* (1997) 59 Cal.App.4th 1241, as modified on denial of reh'g (Jan. 7, 1998), decided under the Berkeley ordinance, not finding preemption by the Ellis Act for the purposes of regulating demolition and historical preservation. See also, *Lincoln Place Tenants Assn. v. City of Los Angeles* (2007) 155 Cal.App.4th 425, as modified on denial of reh'g (Oct. 10, 2007), decided under the Los Angeles ordinance, holding that even under the Ellis Act the developer intended to demolish occupied units still has to comply with CEQA and applicable mitigation measures.

[537] Health and Safety Code section 17980, as explained in *Hawthorne Savings & Loan Assn. v. City of Signal Hill* (1993) 19 Cal.App.4th 148, 160, as modified on denial of reh'g (Nov. 1, 1993).

[538] S.F. Planning Code, Section 317(i)(4).

[539] S.F. Planning Code, Section 317(g)(2) [8 factors considered before a residential merger is allowed]; Sec. 317(g)(3) [6 factors for a residential conversion]; Sec. 317(g)(5) [18 factors for a residential demolition]. See also, Sec. 317(g)(6) [whether to approve removal of unauthorized units].

[540] S.F. Building Code (2016), Section 106A.3.1(10).

[541] See, S.F. Bus. & Tax. Code, Article I, Section 8. S.F. Board of Appeals is vested with the powers to review the building permit under Cal. Gov-t Code § 65903. Belated appeals may also be accepted, if the applicant first applies for the Board's discretion to allow filing of a late appeal and such discretion is granted.

[542] S.F. Rent Board "Fact Sheet 4 – Eviction Issues," "Overview of "Just Cause" Eviction Issues."

[543] S.F. Admin. Code, Sections 37.9(j)(3), first sentence, requires "a written request" or "a notice of termination of tenancy."

[544] S.F. Admin. Code, Section 37.9(j)(3).

[545] S.F. Admin. Code, Section 37.9(h).

[546] 24 CFR 982.310(a)(3) and 24 CFR 982.310(d)(1)(iv).

[547] S.F. Admin. Code, Section 37.3(f)(3).

[548] CC § 1954.535 (part of the Costa-Hawkins Act); S.F. Admin. Code, Section 37.3(d)(3)(A)–(C); S.F. Admin. Code, Section 37.3(f), (f)(1).

NOTES